# TEACHER'S MANUAL
## AND ACHIEVEMENT TESTS

# NORTHSTAR 3
## LISTENING AND SPEAKING

### THIRD EDITION

AUTHORS

**Helen S. Solórzano**
**Jennifer P. L. Schmidt**

SERIES EDITORS

**Frances Boyd**
**Carol Numrich**

PEARSON
Longman

**NorthStar: Listening and Speaking Level 3, Third Edition**
**Teacher's Manual and Achievement Tests**

Pearson Education, 10 Bank Street, White Plains, NY 10606

Teacher's Manual by Gordon Lewis. Activities for secondary schools by Ann Hilborn.

Achievement Tests developed by: Dr. Joan Jamison and Dr. Carol Chapelle.

Achievement Tests by Tony Becker, Maja Grgurovic, and Elizabeth Henly.

Staff credits: The people who made up the *NorthStar: Listening and Speaking Level 3, Third Edition Teacher's Manual* team, representing editorial, production, design, and manufacturing, are Dave Dickey, Christine Edmonds, Ann France, Gosia Jaros-White, Dana Klinek, Melissa Leyva, Sherry Preiss, Robert Ruvo, Debbie Sistino, Jennifer Stem, and Paula Van Ells.

Listening selections and text credits: **Page T-7** Music: Scheming Weasel (slower version), Kevin MacLeod (incompetech.com). Licensed under Creative Commons "Attribution 3.0" http://creativecommons.org/licenses/by/3.0/; **Page T-13** "Ultrarunner Jay Batchen." Podcast presented by www.EndurancePlanet.com. Tim Borquin, host. June 10, 2005; **Page T-29** Audio program that accompanies this text courtesy of Rounder Records, Corp., One Camp Street, Cambridge, Massachusetts 02140 U.S.A.; **Page T-33** "Urban Homesteaders" produced and reported by Karen Brown, WFCR, Amherst, Massachusetts. © 2007 by Karen Brown. Used by permission.

Cover Art: Silvia Rojas/Getty Images
Text composition: ElectraGraphics, Inc.
Text font: 11.5/13 Minion


ISBN-10: 0-13-613314-2
ISBN-13: 978-0-13-613314-8

**PEARSON LONGMAN ON THE WEB**

**Pearsonlongman.com** offers online resources for teachers and students. Access our Companion Websites, our online catalog, and our local offices around the world.

Visit us at **www.pearsonlongman.com**.

Printed in the United States of America
4 5 6 7 8 9 10—HAM—13 12

# CONTENTS

## UNIT-BY-UNIT TEACHING SUGGESTIONS

## ACHIEVEMENT TESTS

# WELCOME TO NORTHSTAR
## THIRD EDITION

*NorthStar*, now in its third edition, motivates students to succeed in their **academic** as well as **personal** language goals.

For each of the five levels, the two strands—*Reading and Writing* and *Listening and Speaking*—provide a fully integrated approach for students and teachers.

## WHAT IS SPECIAL ABOUT THE THIRD EDITION?

### NEW THEMES

**New themes** and **updated content**—presented in a **variety of genres**, including literature and lectures, and in **authentic reading and listening selections**—challenge students intellectually.

### ACADEMIC SKILLS

**More** purposeful **integration of critical thinking** and an enhanced focus on **academic skills** such as inferencing, synthesizing, note taking, and test taking help students develop strategies for **success** in the **classroom** and on **standardized tests**. A **culminating productive task** galvanizes content, language, and **critical thinking skills**.

➤ In the *Listening and Speaking* strand, a **structured approach** gives students opportunities for **more extended and creative oral practice**, for example, presentations, simulations, debates, case studies, and public service announcements.

➤ In the *Reading and Writing* strand, a new, **fully integrated writing section** leads students through the **writing process** with engaging writing assignments focusing on various rhetorical modes.

### NEW DESIGN

Full **color pages** with more **photos, illustrations, and graphic organizers** foster student engagement and make the content and activities come alive.

### MyNorthStarLab

**MyNorthStarLab**, an easy-to-use **online learning and assessment program**, offers:

➤ Unlimited access to reading and listening selections and DVD segments.

➤ Focused test preparation to help students succeed on international exams such as TOEFL® and IELTS®. Pre- and post-unit assessments improve results by providing individualized instruction, instant feedback, and personalized study plans.

➤ Original activities that support and extend the *NorthStar* program. These include pronunciation practice using voice recording tools, and activities to build note taking skills and academic vocabulary.

➤ Tools that save time. These include a flexible gradebook and authoring features that give teachers control of content and help them track student progress.

# THE NORTHSTAR APPROACH

The *NorthStar* series is based on **current research in language acquisition** and on the **experiences of teachers and curriculum designers**. Five principles guide the *NorthStar* approach.

## PRINCIPLES

**1 The more profoundly students are stimulated intellectually and emotionally, the more language they will use and retain.**

The thematic organization of *NorthStar* promotes intellectual and emotional stimulation. The 50 sophisticated themes in *NorthStar* present intriguing topics such as recycled fashion, restorative justice, personal carbon footprints, and microfinance. The authentic content engages students, links them to language use outside of the classroom, and encourages personal expression and critical thinking.

**2 Students can learn both the form and content of the language.**

Grammar, vocabulary, and culture are inextricably woven into the units, providing students with systematic and multiple exposures to language forms in a variety of contexts. As the theme is developed, students can express complex thoughts using a higher level of language.

**3 Successful students are active learners.**

Tasks are designed to be creative, active, and varied. Topics are interesting and up-to-date. Together these tasks and topics (1) allow teachers to bring the outside world into the classroom and (2) motivate students to apply their classroom learning in the outside world.

**4 Students need feedback.**

This feedback comes naturally when students work together practicing language and participating in open-ended opinion and inference tasks. Whole class activities invite teachers' feedback on the spot or via audio/video recordings or notes. The innovative new MyNorthStarLab gives students immediate feedback as they complete computer-graded language activities online; it also gives students the opportunity to submit writing or speaking assignments electronically to their instructor for feedback later.

**5 The quality of relationships in the language classroom is important because students are asked to express themselves on issues and ideas.**

The information and activities in *NorthStar* promote genuine interaction, acceptance of differences, and authentic communication. By building skills and exploring ideas, the exercises help students participate in discussions and write essays of an increasingly complex and sophisticated nature.

# THE NORTHSTAR UNIT

## 1 FOCUS ON THE TOPIC

This section introduces students to the unifying theme of the listening selections.

**PREDICT** and **SHARE INFORMATION** foster interest in the unit topic and help students develop a personal connection to it.

**BACKGROUND AND VOCABULARY** activities provide students with tools for understanding the first listening selection. Later in the unit, students review this vocabulary and learn related idioms, collocations, and word forms. This helps them explore content and expand their written and spoken language.

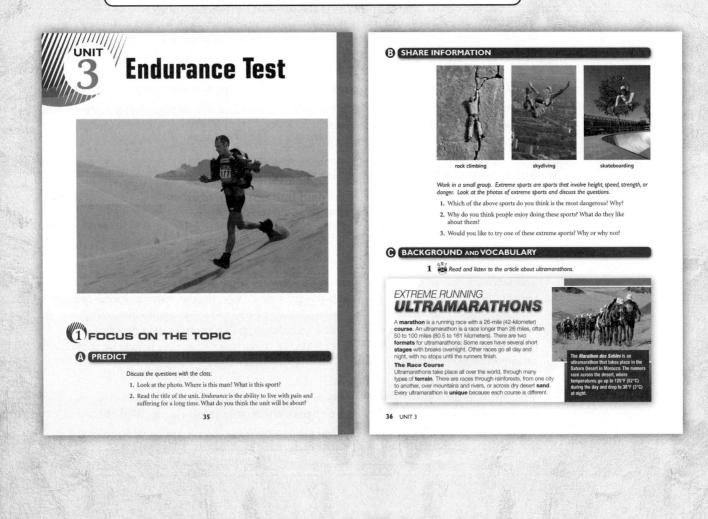

### UNIT 3 — Endurance Test

#### 1 FOCUS ON THE TOPIC

**A PREDICT**

*Discuss the questions with the class.*

1. Look at the photo. Where is this man? What is this sport?
2. Read the title of the unit. *Endurance* is the ability to live with pain and suffering for a long time. What do you think the unit will be about?

35

---

**B SHARE INFORMATION**

rock climbing   skydiving   skateboarding

*Work in a small group. Extreme sports are sports that involve height, speed, strength, or danger. Look at the photos of extreme sports and discuss the questions.*

1. Which of the above sports do you think is the most dangerous? Why?
2. Why do you think people enjoy doing these sports? What do they like about them?
3. Would you like to try one of these extreme sports? Why or why not?

**C BACKGROUND AND VOCABULARY**

1 🎧 Read and listen to the article about ultramarathons.

#### EXTREME RUNNING
#### ULTRAMARATHONS

A **marathon** is a running race with a 26-mile (42-kilometer) **course**. An ultramarathon is a race longer than 26 miles, often 50 to 100 miles (80.5 to 161 kilometers). There are two **formats** for ultramarathons: Some races have several short **stages** with breaks overnight. Other races go all day and night, with no stops until the runners finish.

**The Race Course**

Ultramarathons take place all over the world, through many types of **terrain**. There are races through rainforests, from one city to another, over mountains and rivers, or across dry desert **sand**. Every ultramarathon is **unique** because each course is different.

The *Marathon des Sables* is an ultramarathon that takes place in the Sahara Desert in Morocco. The runners race across the desert, where temperatures go up to 125°F (52°C) during the day and drop to 38°F (3°C) at night.

36   UNIT 3

---

**FOCUS ON LISTENING**

This section focuses on understanding two contrasting listening selections.

**LISTENING ONE** is a radio report, interview, lecture, or other genre that addresses the unit topic. In levels 1 to 3, listenings are based on authentic materials. In levels 4 and 5, all the listenings are authentic.

**LISTEN FOR MAIN IDEAS** and **LISTEN FOR DETAILS** are comprehension activities that lead students to an understanding and appreciation of the first selection.

The **MAKE INFERENCES** activity prompts students to "listen between the lines," move beyond the literal meaning, exercise critical thinking skills, and understand the listening on a more academic level. Students follow up with pair or group work to discuss topics in the **EXPRESS OPINIONS** section.

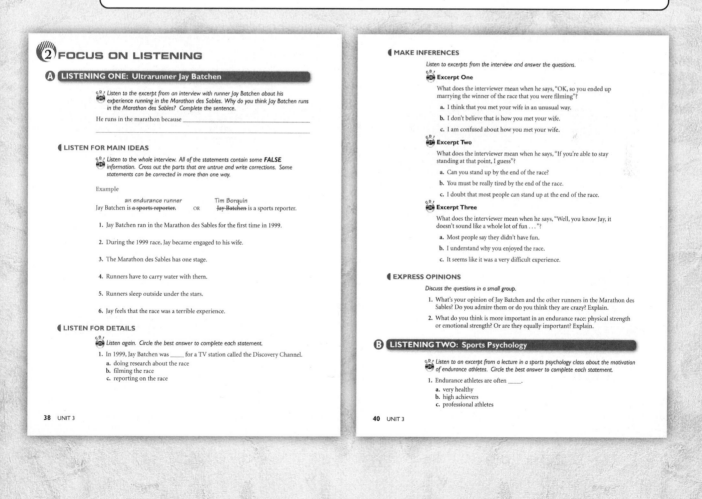

**② FOCUS ON LISTENING**

**A ⬛ LISTENING ONE: Ultrarunner Jay Batchen**

🎧 *Listen to the excerpt from an interview with runner Jay Batchen about his experience running in the Marathon des Sables. Why do you think Jay Batchen runs in the Marathon des Sables? Complete the sentence.*

He runs in the marathon because _____

**◀ LISTEN FOR MAIN IDEAS**

🎧 *Listen to the whole interview. All of the statements contain some **FALSE** information. Cross out the parts that are untrue and write corrections. Some statements can be corrected in more than one way.*

Example

     an endurance runner    Tim Borquin
Jay Batchen is ~~a sports reporter.~~  OR  ~~Jay Batchen~~ is a sports reporter.

1. Jay Batchen ran in the Marathon des Sables for the first time in 1999.

2. During the 1999 race, Jay became engaged to his wife.

3. The Marathon des Sables has one stage.

4. Runners have to carry water with them.

5. Runners sleep outside under the stars.

6. Jay feels that the race was a terrible experience.

**◀ LISTEN FOR DETAILS**

🎧 *Listen again. Circle the best answer to complete each statement.*

1. In 1999, Jay Batchen was _____ for a TV station called the Discovery Channel.
 **a.** doing research about the race
 **b.** filming the race
 **c.** reporting on the race

**38** UNIT 3

**◀ MAKE INFERENCES**

*Listen to excerpts from the interview and answer the questions.*

🎧 **Excerpt One**

What does the interviewer mean when he says, "OK, so you ended up marrying the winner of the race that you were filming"?

 **a.** I think that you met your wife in an unusual way.

 **b.** I don't believe that is how you met your wife.

 **c.** I am confused about how you met your wife.

🎧 **Excerpt Two**

What does the interviewer mean when he says, "If you're able to stay standing at that point, I guess"?

 **a.** Can you stand up by the end of the race?

 **b.** You must be really tired by the end of the race.

 **c.** I doubt that most people can stand up at the end of the race.

🎧 **Excerpt Three**

What does the interviewer mean when he says, "Well, you know Jay, it doesn't sound like a whole lot of fun . . ."?

 **a.** Most people say they didn't have fun.

 **b.** I understand why you enjoyed the race.

 **c.** It seems like it was a very difficult experience.

**◀ EXPRESS OPINIONS**

*Discuss the questions in a small group.*

1. What's your opinion of Jay Batchen and the other runners in the Marathon des Sables? Do you admire them or do you think they are crazy? Explain.

2. What do you think is more important in an endurance race: physical strength or emotional strength? Or are they equally important? Explain.

**B ⬛ LISTENING TWO: Sports Psychology**

🎧 *Listen to an excerpt from a lecture in a sports psychology class about the motivation of endurance athletes. Circle the best answer to complete each statement.*

1. Endurance athletes are often _____.
 **a.** very healthy
 **b.** high achievers
 **c.** professional athletes

**40** UNIT 3

**LISTENING TWO** offers another perspective on the topic and is usually another genre. Again, in levels 1 to 3, the listenings are based on authentic materials and in levels 4 and 5, they are authentic. This second listening is followed by an activity that challenges students to question ideas they formed about the first listening, and to use appropriate language skills to analyze and explain their ideas.

**INTEGRATE LISTENINGS ONE AND TWO** presents culminating activities. Students are challenged to take what they have learned, organize the information, and synthesize it in a meaningful way. Students practice skills that are essential for success in authentic academic settings and on standardized tests.

---

**B** **LISTENING TWO: Simple Gifts**

**1** *Read the information about the Shakers, an eighteenth-century religious group who chose to live simply.*

The Shakers were a religious group that formed in Britain in the 1700s. They came to the United States so they could be free to practice their religion.

The Shakers believed that simple living would make them happy and would bring them closer to God. They wore plain clothing and shared everything. They never married or had children. Men and women lived in separate houses.

The name "Shakers" came from the group's style of dancing. Dancing was an important part of Shaker religion. However, other people thought the Shaker dances were very strange.

"Simple Gifts" is a Shaker dance song written in 1848 that is still a popular folk song today.

**2** 🎵 Listen to the song. Complete the song lyrics with the missing words from the box. Some words are used twice. Listen again if you need to.

| | | | |
|---|---|---|---|
| ashamed | delight | gained | ~~simple~~ |
| be | free | right | |

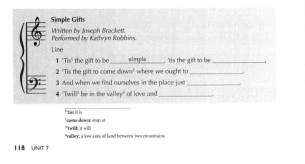

**Simple Gifts**

*Written by Joseph Brackett.*
*Performed by Kathryn Robbins.*

Line

1 'Tis[1] the gift to be ___simple___, 'tis the gift to be _____,

2 'Tis the gift to come down[2] where we ought to _____,

3 And when we find ourselves in the place just _____,

4 'Twill[3] be in the valley[4] of love and _____.

---
[1]**'tis:** it is
[2]**come down:** stop at
[3]**'twill:** it will
[4]**valley:** a low area of land between two mountains

---

**C** **INTEGRATE LISTENINGS ONE AND TWO**

**STEP 1: Organize**

There are connections between the ideas in the Shaker song "Simple Gifts" and the lifestyle of the urban homesteaders. Work with a partner. Read the lines from the song. Then answer the questions.

| LINES FROM "SIMPLE GIFTS" | QUESTIONS | ANSWERS FOR URBAN HOMESTEADERS |
|---|---|---|
| 'Tis the gift to be simple. | 1. What do the urban homesteaders do to lead a simple life? | they grow their own vegetables |
| 'Tis the gift to be free. | 2. In what ways are the urban homesteaders free? (What things are they free from?) | |
| 'Tis the gift to come down where we ought to be. | 3. Why is the inner city the place where the urban homesteaders want to be? | |
| 'Twill be in the valley of love and delight. | 4. What makes the urban homesteaders delighted (happy)? | |

**STEP 2: Synthesize**

Work with a new partner and compare your answers to the questions. Take turns reading the questions and responding by agreeing, disagreeing, or adding more information. Use the information from Step 1 and the useful language on the next page.

Example

STUDENT A: OK. Question 1 says, "What do the urban homesteaders do to lead a simple life?" Well . . . to lead a simple life the urban homesteaders grow their own vegetables.

STUDENT B: Right. They also don't use electricity.

---

# ③ FOCUS ON SPEAKING

This section emphasizes development of productive skills for speaking. It includes sections on vocabulary, grammar, pronunciation, functional language, and an extended speaking task.

> The **VOCABULARY** section leads students from reviewing the unit vocabulary, to practicing and expanding their use of it, and then working with it—using it creatively in both this section and in the final speaking task.
>
> Students learn useful structures for speaking in the **GRAMMAR** section, which offers a concise presentation and targeted practice. Vocabulary items are recycled here, providing multiple exposures leading to mastery. For additional practice with the grammar presented, students and teachers can consult the GRAMMAR BOOK REFERENCES at the end of the book for corresponding material in the *Focus on Grammar* and Azar series.

---

## ③ FOCUS ON SPEAKING

### A VOCABULARY

#### ◖ REVIEW

*Cross out the word that doesn't belong in each group. Consult a dictionary if necessary.*

Example

| | | | |
|---|---|---|---|
| zoo | ~~museum~~ | animal park | wildlife center |
| 1. afford | have money for | pay for | borrow from |
| 2. controversy | argument | debate | agreement |
| 3. depend on | rely on | need | choose |
| 4. degrading | polite | embarrassing | painful |
| 5. make a living | earn money | enjoy life | get paid |
| 6. preserve | destroy | save | care for |
| 7. season | days of the week | time of year | period of time |
| 8. souvenir | reminder | keepsake | equipment |
| 9. stretch | enlarge | make longer | reduce |
| 10. tourist attraction | place to see | guidebook | point of interest |
| 11. tradition | habit | change | belief |
| 12. village | small town | community | city |
| 13. wrap | open | cover | surround |

#### ◖ EXPAND

**1** *Read the letter to the editor about the effects of tourism in Cape Cod.*

---
**TO THE EDITOR:**

*Effects of Tourism*

Millions of tourists visit Cape Cod each year. Most tourists come here to relax at the beach and enjoy our delicious seafood. Others like to **get off the beaten path** and explore parts of the Cape that most tourists don't see. Whatever they do here, we appreciate the tourists because most **locals** have jobs that depend on tourism, such as shop owners and restaurant workers.

*(continued on next page)*

---

Culture and Commerce **81**

### B GRAMMAR: Future Predictions with *If*-clauses

**1** *Work with a partner. Read the conversation between two residents of Cape Cod. Then switch roles and repeat.*

A: Did you see the weather report today? They say it**'ll** keep raining all week.
B: Really? That's bad. **If it keeps raining**, the tourists **won't** come. They**'ll** stay home.
A: I know. I**'ll probably** lose money this week.

| FUTURE PREDICTIONS WITH *IF*-CLAUSES | |
|---|---|
| **1.** Use **will** + base form and **will not** (**won't**) + base form to make predictions about the future.<br><br>**Will** is usually contracted in speech. | It **will rain** again next week.<br><br>Tourists **won't come** to the shops and restaurants.<br><br>They**'ll stay** home. |
| **2.** Use **probably** with **will**.<br><br>**Probably** comes between **will** and the main verb.<br><br>In a negative sentence, **probably** comes before **won't**. | Business **will probably be** slow all week.<br><br>I **probably won't make** enough money. |
| **3.** Use **if-clauses** to talk about possible results in the future.<br><br>In the main clause, use **will** + base form. In the **if-clause**, use simple present.<br><br>The **if-clause** can come before or after the main clause. When it comes first, use a comma between the clauses. | If the rain **continues**, we**'ll have** a lot of problems.<br>　*if-clause*　　　　*main clause*<br><br>We**'ll have** a lot of problems if the rain **continues**.<br>　　*main clause*　　　　　*if-clause* |

**2** *Complete the sentences using the words in parentheses. Use contractions of **will** where possible.*

1. If it ___rains___ a lot this summer, fewer tourists ___will visit___.
   　　　(rain)　　　　　　　　　　　　　　　　　　(visit)

   Businesses ___probably won't make___ enough money. Some shops
   　　　　　　(probably / not / make)

   ___will probably close___.
   　　(probably / close)

Culture and Commerce **83**

The **PRONUNCIATION** section presents both controlled and freer, communicative practice of the sounds and patterns of English. Models from the listening selections reinforce content and vocabulary. This is followed by the **FUNCTION** section where students are exposed to functional language that prepares them to express ideas on a higher level. Examples have been chosen based on frequency, variety, and usefulness for the final speaking task.

The **PRODUCTION** section gives students an opportunity to integrate the ideas, vocabulary, grammar, pronunciation, and function presented in the unit. This final speaking task is the culminating activity of the unit and gets students to exchange ideas and express opinions in sustained speaking contexts. Activities are presented in a sequence that builds confidence and fluency, and allows for more than one "try" at expression. When appropriate, students practice some presentation skills: audience analysis, organization, eye contact, or use of visuals.

---

## C SPEAKING

### ◀ PRONUNCIATION: Rhythm of Prepositional Phrases

A prepositional phrase consists of a preposition (P) and a noun phrase (NP).

Example
P    NP
They drove to the social.

| RHYTHM OF PREPOSITIONAL PHRASES | |
|---|---|
| Short prepositions: to, at, in, of, on, with, for, from are not stressed in prepositional phrases. | Lavender rode in their car. <br><br> They danced with Lavender. |
| Unstressed prepositions join closely to the other words in a prepositional phrase. (In the example, the prepositional phrases and single words have the same stress pattern.) | for breakfast    forbidden <br><br> in the rain    unafraid |
| Some prepositions have reduced pronunciations: The vowel is pronounced /ə/ in speaking. | at home    /ət/ <br><br> for dinner    /fər/; rhymes with her <br><br> to school    to is usually /tə/; sounds like t'school <br><br> in town    /ən/ or /ɪn/ |

**1** 🔊 Listen to the sentences. *Complete the sentences with the prepositions you hear.*

1. Robert and David drove _____ their house.
2. Lavender was waiting _____ the road.
3. She walked _____ Robert.
4. The three friends went _____ the dance.
5. They got back _____ the car.
6. Robert and David were looking _____ the coat in the backyard.
7. Robert pointed _____ the gravestone.
8. They ran _____ the car.

*Compare your answers with a partner's. Take turns saying the sentences aloud. Try to use the /ə/ sound when appropriate.*

---

### ◀ PRODUCTION: Telling a Story

In this activity, you will **prepare a story and tell it to the class**. The story could be from your culture or one that you make up yourself. Try to use the vocabulary, grammar, pronunciation, and transitions you learned in the unit.*

*Follow the steps.*

**Step 1:** Think of a short story that will be interesting and entertaining for your audience. It could be exciting, scary, funny, or sad. It could have unexpected events or a moral, or it could have unusual characters.

Write an outline of your story on a piece of paper. Use the sample outline as a guide.

Title of the story: _____

Place where the story takes place: _____

**Main characters** (name and description):

1. _____
2. _____
3. _____
Etc.

**Outline of events** (List the main events using words and phrases):

1. _____
2. _____
3. _____
Etc.

**Step 2:** Use your outline to practice your story. Use the storytelling techniques discussed in this unit.

• Use your voice (loud / soft, high / low) to create feelings.
• Use dialogue to bring your characters to life.

After you have practiced on your own, meet with a partner and tell your story. Switch partners and tell your story again.

**Step 3:** Perform your story for the class. Be dramatic and have fun.

_____
*For Alternative Speaking Topics, see page 109.

---

**ALTERNATIVE SPEAKING TOPICS** are provided at the end of the unit. They can be used as alternatives to the final speaking task, or as *additional* assignments. RESEARCH TOPICS tied to the theme of the unit are organized in a special section at the back of the book.

# MyNorthStarLab

**MyNorthStarLab** supports students with **individualized instruction**, **feedback**, and **extra help**. A wide array of resources, including a flexible **gradebook**, helps teachers manage student progress.

The MyNorthStarLab **WELCOME** page **organizes assignments and grades**, and **facilitates communication** between students and teachers.

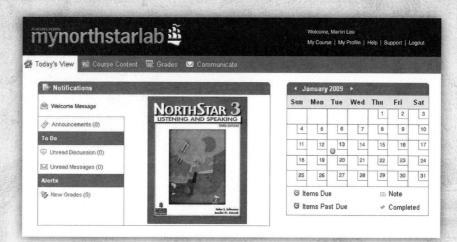

For each unit, MyNorthStarLab provides a **READINESS CHECK**.

➤ Activities **assess** student knowledge **before** beginning the unit and **follow up** with individualized instruction.

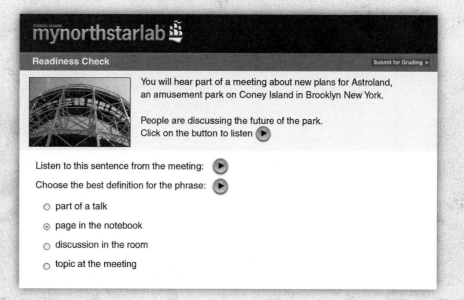

Student book material and **new** practice activities are available to students online.

➤ Students benefit from virtually unlimited **practice anywhere, anytime**.

Interaction with **Internet** and **video** materials will:

➤ Expand students' knowledge of the topic.

➤ Help students practice new vocabulary and grammar.

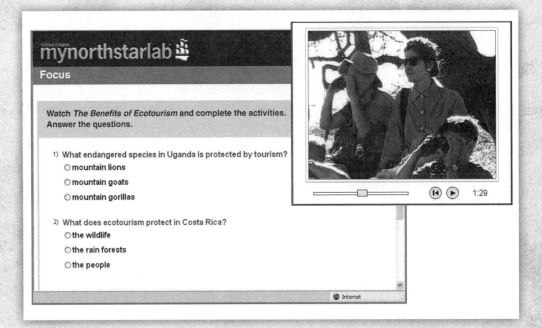

**INTEGRATED SKILL ACTIVITIES** in MyNorthStarLab challenge students to bring together the **language skills** and **critical thinking skills** that they have practiced throughout the unit.

The MyNorthStarLab **ASSESSMENT** tools allow instructors to customize and deliver achievement tests online.

---

mynorthstarlab

Integrated Task - Read, Listen, Write                                   Submit for Grading ▶

### THE ADVENTURE OF A LIFETIME

We at the Antarctic Travel Society encourage you to consider an excited guided tour of Antarctica for your next vacation.

The Antarctic Travel society carefully plans and operates tours of the Antarctic by ship. There are three trips per day leaving from ports in South America and Australia. Each ship carries only about 100 passengers at a time. Tours run from November through March to the ice-free areas along the coast of Antarctica.

In addition to touring the coast, our ships stop for on-land visits, which generally last for about three hours. Activities include guided sightseeing, mountain climbing, camping, kayaking, and scuba diving. For a longer stay, camping trips can also be arranged.

Our tours will give you an opportunity to experience the richness of Antarctica, including its wildlife, history, active research stations, and, most of all, its natural beauty.

Tours are supervised by the ship's staff. The staff generally includes experts in animal and sea life and other Antarctica specialists. There is generally one staff member for every 10 to 20 passengers. Theses trained and responsible individuals will help to make your visit to Antarctica safe, educational, and unforgettable.

**READ, LISTEN AND WRITE ABOUT TOURISM IN ANTARCTICA**
Read.
Read the text. Then answer the question.

According to the text, how can tourism benefit the Antarctic?

Listen.
Click on the Play button and listen to the passage. Use the outline to take notes as you listen.

Main idea:

Seven things that scientists study:

The effects of tourism:

Write.
Write about the potential and risks in Antarctica.
Follow the steps to prepare.

**Step 1**
• Review the text and your outline from the listening task.
• Write notes about the benefits and risks of tourism.

**Step 2**
Write for 20 minutes. Leave 5 minutes to edit your work.

---

mynorthstarlab

Welcome, Martin Lee
My Course | My Profile | Help | Support | Logout

**Student Course > Achievement Test**
To begin, open the Skills Check. After you submit the test, you will return to this screen. If y
you will be assigned study material to help with your learning.

**Skills Check**
Vocabulary

Your score: 72%

**Study Material**
Part 2: Vocabulary
Pass Criteria: 75%

Name
Vocabulary: Exercise 1
Vocabulary: Exercise 2

**Vocabulary Exercise 1**
Click on the box next to the vocabulary word to match its definition.

1) controversy

an argument about opposing opinions
protect something from harm
a cultural practice or custom
a small community of houses
a park where living animals are kept
a reminder of a place visited

2) zoo

Hints    Hint 1

---

mynorthstarlab

Your Score: 80%

Listen to the beginning of a news report about Thailand. Choose the best prediction of what the news report will contain. There is only one right answer.

✗ information about religious holidays
○ information about celebrating elephants
○ information about tourist travel
○ information about the national flag

Answer(s):    information about celebrating elephants
Feedback:    The speaker says:
One might wonder—why celebrate a holiday in honor of the elephant?
Click on the audio button to listen. 🔊

# OVERVIEW OF THE TEACHER'S MANUAL AND ACHIEVEMENT TESTS

The **NorthStar Teacher's Manual** includes:

➤ Specific suggestions for teaching each unit

➤ Student Book Answer Key

➤ An alphabetized-by-unit word list of the key vocabulary items practiced in each unit

➤ Reproducible Achievement Tests with Answer Keys—including the test audioscript and test audio CD

# UNIT-BY-UNIT TEACHING SUGGESTIONS

Unit-by-unit overview (scope and sequence), list of skills practiced in each section of the student book, suggested teaching times, teaching suggestions, suggestions on how to use *NorthStar* in secondary classes, Expansion/Homework activities, cross-references to the companion strand, techniques and instructions for using MyNorthStarLab

---

## UNIT 9 — Personal Carbon Footprint

### OVERVIEW

**Theme:** Climate change
This unit focuses on the issue of global warming from a personal perspective. Students explore reasons for global warming and discuss how individual action to reduce one's carbon footprint can have an impact on climate change. Students also analyze graphs and data related to global warming, and participate in a seminar discussing the issue.

**Listening One:** *Personal Carbon Footprint* is a radio report describing one approach to offsetting one's personal carbon footprint.

**Listening Two:** *A Call to Action* is a speech by an activist at an environmental rally.

### Critical Thinking

| | |
|---|---|
| Interpret illustrations | Classify data |
| Complete a survey on personal carbon footprints | Categorize information |
| Understand a scientific process | Read a map |
| Infer word meaning from context | Interpret a graph |

### Listening

| | |
|---|---|
| Predict content | Label a graph |
| Listen for main ideas | Organize and synthesize information from the |
| Listen for details | listenings |
| Infer speakers' opinions | |

### Speaking

| | |
|---|---|
| Speculate about the content of the unit | Agree and disagree with statements |
| Discuss results of a survey | Interrupt politely and hold the floor |
| Express and defend opinions | Participate in a seminar about climate change |

| Vocabulary | Grammar |
|---|---|
| Use context clues to find meaning | Modals of necessity |
| Define words | **Pronunciation** |
| Identify and use correct word forms | Intonation—Are you finished? |

📁 **MyNorthStarLab**
Readiness Check, Background and Vocabulary, Listenings One and Two, Notetaking and Academic Skills Practice, Vocabulary and Grammar, Achievement Test

🎧 *NorthStar: Reading and Writing 3*
Unit 9 explores the topic of global warming and international and national government policy on climate change.

85

---

3. Have students complete **Exercise 2** in pairs or individually. Then review the answers with the class. Have students point out words or phrases in the article that helped them guess the correct meaning of the words in the exercise.

🎧 **Link to *NorthStar: Reading and Writing 3***
If students are also using the companion text, you may want to list vocabulary from Background and Vocabulary, pages 20–21, on the board and see if students can find synonyms for those words in the background passage.

📁 Go to www.mynorthstarlab.com for additional *Background and Vocabulary* practice.

## ② FOCUS ON LISTENING

### ◖ SKILLS

Predict the content of a passage; listen for main ideas; identify details; infer information through intonation; express opinions about information in the listening; listen to and discuss Public Service Announcements.

### ◦◦◦ Ⓐ LISTENING ONE: Lily's Story

📁 Go to www.mynorthstarlab.com to listen to *Lily's Story*.

**Suggested Time: 5 minutes**

In Listening One, students listen to a woman describe her experiences with identity theft and how it affected her life.

1. Read the introduction with the class. Then play the audio and have students circle the correct answer.

2. Go over the answer with the class. Have students explain their choices.

### LISTENING STRATEGY: Set a Purpose for Listening

1. Discuss why and how we listen. Ask students to brainstorm a list of things we listen to (music, lecture, conversations) and then ask if we listen to all of these in the same way. Write students' ideas on the board.

2. After the list is complete, help students classify the ideas into one of the following categories: to get information, to solve problems, to enjoy, to evaluate. Students might wish to add items as you organize the information. Then have students speculate as to how we might listen differently for each category (for example, information—we might listen more closely to details or we might take notes).

14   UNIT 2

# USING *NORTHSTAR* IN SECONDARY CLASSES

Each unit of the *Teacher's Manual* offers a set of strategies that provide opportunities for greater differentiation in a typical mixed classroom to meet the needs of multi-level secondary students. These strategies are equally beneficial in academic and adult classes. The scaffolded instruction enables teachers to facilitate student mastery of complex skills and ideas. Repeated exposure to concepts helps accelerate English language learning.

**Reading/Listening Strategies** give teachers additional support to guide students who have limited experience with basic reading/listening skills as they learn to explore and understand academic content. Suggestions are given to help students understand how to predict, determine main idea and supporting details, navigate and comprehend a text, monitor their understanding, and organize information.

**Reaching All Students** are activity suggestions for two levels of language proficiency, intended to assist less proficient students and challenge students with higher proficiencies. These are generally included in the Reading/Listening section to help teachers to modify reading/listening activities.

**Critical Thinking** suggestions focus on a hierarchy of questions using Bloom's taxonomy. These are designed specifically to scaffold questions to move students from knowledge-based questions to higher order thinking.

**Vocabulary Expansion** builds upon vocabulary introduced in each unit to help students further integrate vocabulary. They are offered as word analysis or as vocabulary strategies to reinforce vocabulary skills and provide opportunities for review.

# COURSE PLANNERS

Each unit contains approximately eight hours of classroom material, plus expansion, homework, and support material, including MyNorthStarLab. Teachers can customize the units by assigning some exercises for homework and/or eliminating others. To help teachers customize the units for their specific teaching situation, the unit-by-unit teaching suggestions in the *Teacher's Manual* include 1, 2, or 3 stars to indicate the relative importance of each section or exercise as follows:

✪✪✪ **Essential:** Predict, Background and Vocabulary, Listening One, Listen for Main Ideas, Listen for Details, Make Inferences, Express Opinions, Listening Two, Integrate Listenings One and Two, Production

✪✪ **Recommended:** Share Information, Expand, Grammar, Pronunciation, Function

✪ **Optional:** Review, Create, Speaking Topics, Research Topics

| Class time available per unit | Sections to complete |
|---|---|
| 8 hours or more | Essential (✪✪✪), Recommended (✪✪), Optional (✪) |
| 6 hours | Essential (✪✪✪), Recommended (✪✪) |
| 4 hours | Essential (✪✪✪) only |

For more detailed, downloadable unit-by-unit course planners, visit www.mynorthstarlab.com or www.longman.com/northstar.

# ACHIEVEMENT TESTS

The reproducible Achievement Tests allow teachers to evaluate students' progress and to identify areas where students might have problems developing their listening and speaking skills. The Achievement Tests should be given upon completion of the corresponding unit.

## Description

There are four parts for every test:

**Parts 1** and **2** test students' receptive skills. Part 1 assesses students' mastery of listening comprehension. **Part 2** assesses the knowledge of the vocabulary introduced in the unit. **Parts 3** and **4** test students' productive skills. Part 3 assesses students' knowledge of the grammar, pronunciation, and functions introduced in the unit. Part 4 is a speaking test related to the content of the unit.

## Administration

All parts of each test should be taken in class and students should not be allowed access to any *NorthStar* materials or to their dictionaries. Students should be able to complete Parts 1–3 within 40 minutes and Part 4 within 10 minutes.

Teachers can decide how to incorporate Part 4 (the speaking task) into their testing situations. Some teachers will assign each speaking task immediately after students complete Parts 1–3; others may decide to set aside another time to complete it.

## Scoring the Parts

**Parts 1–3:** Individual test items are worth one point, for a maximum total of 30 points per test. A student's raw score can be obtained by adding together the number of correct items, or by subtracting the total number of incorrect items from 30. To convert the raw score to a percentage score, multiply it by 3.33.

**Part 4:** The speaking tasks are evaluated based on speaking skills and function. There are two shorter test items in this part, each worth one point. These should be scored according to the suggestions provided in the answer key for each test. The extended speaking tasks are evaluated holistically using scoring rubrics. The scale ranges from 0–4 and includes information from the listening and fluency/pronunciation, connectedness, structures and vocabulary from the unit, and errors.

**Combining scores from Parts 1–3 and Part 4:** To get a total Achievement Test score, multiply the extended speaking task score by 2. Add the score for the shorter speaking items to this score for the extended speaking task. Then, add the score in Parts 1–3. Multiply this new score by 2.5 to get a percentage score.

| Example 1 | Example 2 |
|---|---|
| Score on Test Parts 1–3 = 30 | Score on Parts 1–3 = 25 |
| Score on Part 4 (extended task) = 4 | Score on Part 4 (extended task) = 2 |
| Multiply 4 x 2 | Multiply 2 x 2 |
| Score on Part 4 (shorter items) = 2 | Score on Part 4 (shorter items) = 1 |
| Add 10 to 30 | Add 5 to 25 |
| Multiply 40 x 2.5 | Multiply 30 by 2.5 |
| Total score = 100% | Total score = 72.5% |

## Using the Scoring Rubrics

The *NorthStar Listening and Speaking* rubrics are adapted from the integrated speaking rubric of TOEFL iBT. Whereas the TOEFL iBT scoring rubric is intended to distinguish levels of English proficiency among candidates to colleges and universities, the *NorthStar* scoring rubrics are intended to show progress in students' speaking at each of the five *NorthStar* levels. Therefore, *NorthStar* scoring bands make finer distinctions than TOEFL iBT's scoring band. In this way, students at each level will be able to both see improvement in their scores and receive high marks. The detailed scoring rubric is included in the Achievement Tests Answer Key.

| Relationship between TOEFL iBT Rubric and *NorthStar 3* Integrated Speaking Rubric | | |
|:---:|:---:|:---:|
| **TOEFL iBT** | | *NorthStar 3* |
| 3 | | 4 |
| 3 | | 3 |
| 2 | | 2 |
| 2 | | 1 |
| 1 | | 0 |
| 0 | | |

# OTHER NORTHSTAR COMPONENTS

## EXAMVIEW

*NorthStar* ExamView is a stand-alone CD-ROM that allows teachers to **create and customize** their own *NorthStar* tests.

## DVD

The *NorthStar* DVD has **engaging, authentic video clips**, including animation, documentaries, interviews, and biographies, that correspond to the themes in *NorthStar*. Each theme contains a three- to five-minute segment that can be used with either the *Reading and Writing* strand or the *Listening and Speaking* strand. The video clips can also be viewed in MyNorthStarLab.

## COMPANION WEBSITE

The companion website, www.longman.com/northstar, includes resources for teachers, such as the scope and sequence, correlations to other Longman products and to state standards, and podcasts from the *NorthStar* authors and series editors.

# UNIT 1 Advertising on the Air

| OVERVIEW |
| --- |

**Theme:** Advertising
This unit explores the topic of advertising and advertising techniques companies use to sell their products. Students analyze ads and share their knowledge and opinions of advertising, and use the information from the unit to create, perform, and evaluate ads.

**Listening One:** *Advertising on the Air* is a lecture from an introductory business course on advertising.

**Listening Two:** *Negative Appeals* presents radio ads using negative appeals.

## Critical Thinking

Interpret and critique ads
Infer word meaning from context
Classify information

Identify salient features of an ad
Support answers with details from the listenings
Identify intended market of ads

## Listening

Predict content
Listen for main ideas
Identify supporting details
Infer underlying messages in ads

Organize and synthesize information from the listenings
Identify emphasis in speech
Evaluate effectiveness of ads
Listen to and evaluate student ads

## Speaking

Speculate about the content of the unit
Comment on ads using new vocabulary
Share personal opinions about advertising
Use appropriate stress and intonation

Use attention-grabbing language to promote a product
Create, rehearse, and perform an ad

### Vocabulary

Use context clues to find meaning
Identify parts of speech
Choose word definitions

### Grammar

Present simple and present progressive

### Pronunciation

Highlighting words

📁 *MyNorthStarLab*
Readiness Check, Background and Vocabulary, Listenings One and Two, Notetaking and Academic Skills Practice, Vocabulary and Grammar, Achievement Test

🔗 *NorthStar: Reading and Writing 3*
Unit 1 focuses on global advertising and the challenges of tailoring advertising messages to specific markets.

1

# ① FOCUS ON THE TOPIC

## ◖ SKILLS

Interpret an ad; predict unit content based on the photograph and unit title; share personal knowledge and opinions of ads; infer meaning of new vocabulary from context.

## ✿✿✿ Ⓐ PREDICT

**Suggested Time: 5 minutes**

1. Have students look at the ad and suggest products for question 1. List the suggestions on the board. Then have the students check the answer listed on the bottom of the page.

2. Discuss question 2 with the students. Have them discuss whether the ad is effective in advertising a pain medication.

3. While discussing question 3, have students guess the meaning of *on the air* and explain if necessary.

**Expansion/Homework**
Brainstorm other types of advertising. Have students list other types of advertising "on the air" besides radio (TV, Internet).

## ✿✿ Ⓑ SHARE INFORMATION

**Suggested Time: 15 minutes**

Have students work in small groups to describe ads they have seen and heard recently. The ads can be English language or from students' home country. Move around the room and listen to the discussions. Encourage students to use the target questions to guide their discussion.

## ✿✿✿ Ⓒ BACKGROUND AND VOCABULARY

 Go to www.mynorthstarlab.com for *Background and Vocabulary*.

**Suggested Time: 20 minutes**

1. Tell students they will read and listen to an article on advertising. Play the recording of the article in **Exercise 1** and have students listen as they read.

**2.** Have students complete **Exercise 2** in pairs or individually. Then review the answers with the class.

**3.** Have students point out words or phrases in the article that helped them guess the correct meaning of the words in the exercise.

Go to www.mynorthstarlab.com for additional *Background and Vocabulary* practice.

# FOCUS ON LISTENING

## ◖ SKILLS

Predict the content of a passage; listen for main ideas; identify details; infer underlying messages in ads; express opinions about the effectiveness of ads; listen to and interpret ads.

## ✪✪✪ Ⓐ LISTENING ONE: Advertising on the Air

Go to www.mynorthstarlab.com to listen to *Advertising on the Air.*

**Suggested Time: 5 minutes**

In Listening One, students hear a lecture by a professor describing emotional appeals in advertising. Students listen to identify emotional appeals in ads and familiarize themselves with a lecture format.

**1.** Play the excerpt from the lecture. Have students complete the sentence with their prediction of the topic of the lecture.

**2.** Ask students to share their predictions with the class. Affirm each prediction as a possibility.

### LISTENING STRATEGY: Preview

**1.** Tell students that academic lectures are usually aligned with a textbook chapter or unit, and that their ability to listen to and understand the lecture can be improved if they take the time to preview the unit prior to the lecture.

**2.** Model how students can preview the unit by looking at titles, subheadings, illustrations, and vocabulary to gain some general information before they listen. Then ask them to use the information from the preview and share with a partner what they think *on the air* means and what they think the lecture is about.

### ✪✪✪ LISTEN FOR MAIN IDEAS                      **Suggested Time: 15 minutes**

**1.** Play the lecture without pausing and have students complete the exercise.

**2.** Go over the answers with the class.

- **Less Proficient:** Invite students to look for humorous and/or informational ads in magazines to discuss with their partner and share with the class.

- **More Proficient:** Have students work with a partner to storyboard images of what they heard.

## ✪✪✪ LISTEN FOR DETAILS                    Suggested Time: 15 minutes

1. Have students look at the notes. Tell them that they will complete the notes with the information from the lecture.

2. Play the lecture one more time and have students listen and fill in the gaps.

3. Have students compare their answers with a partner's. Then call on individual students to share their answers with the entire class. If there are differences of opinion, you can replay relevant portions of the lecture.

## ✪✪✪ MAKE INFERENCES                       Suggested Time: 15 minutes

1. Explain that ads are designed based on certain ideas about consumers. Tell students that they will listen to two radio ads and must guess what these ideas are. Have students complete the exercise.

2. Have students discuss their answers in small groups. Move around the room and listen in, commenting where appropriate.

3. Go over the answers with the class. Encourage students to support their answers with information from the audio. Emphasize that it's possible for students to have varying opinions as long as their reasoning is sound.

## ✪✪✪ EXPRESS OPINIONS                      Suggested Time: 15 minutes

1. Place students in small groups. Have each student evaluate the ads using the scale and discuss their opinions with the other students in the group.

2. Bring the class together and survey the answers with a show of hands. Is there any consensus? Invite individual students to explain their opinions of the ads.

3. Discuss question 2 with the whole class. Write students' ideas on the board.

**Expansion/Homework**
Ask students how the ads would be different on the Internet. Bring up multimedia and interactivity. Invite students to bring in print or Internet ads for classmates to rate according to the criteria in Exercise 1.

# CRITICAL THINKING

Give students the following questions for discussion in small groups before discussing as a whole class:

1. What is an advertiser's number one problem?

   Answer: Getting the consumer's attention.

2. What are the methods advertisers use to get our attention?

   Answer: Students can respond using information from the lecture (appeals to information and emotion) and from their own experience and knowledge.

3. In addition to the "feel good factor," why do you think humor is effective in ads?

   Answers will vary, but might include that they're attention getting, interesting, entertaining, and therefore cause us to remember. Students should provide evidence to support their responses.

4. How can you use this knowledge about advertising in your own life?

   Answers will vary, but might include that awareness of advertising methods will help them to be more discriminating in their purchases and more aware of the potential power of advertising.

## ✪✪✪ B  LISTENING TWO: Negative Appeals

Go to www.mynorthstarlab.com to listen to *Negative Appeals*.

**Suggested Time: 10 minutes**

Listening Two presents additional radio ads. Students listen to identify negative emotions used to advertise a product.

1. Introduce the concept of negative emotions. Explain that negative emotions are emotions that make people have unpleasant feelings such as sadness, embarrassment, or fear. Then review the vocabulary in the box.

2. Review the instructions for the activity and play the ads. Have students complete the chart. Invite individual students to share their results for each ad. Encourage discussion.

**Expansion/Homework**
Have students brainstorm additional negative emotions. They can also look for synonyms, antonyms, and alternative word forms and add them to their vocabulary notebooks.

◖ **SKILLS**

Define concepts and provide examples from the listenings; organize and synthesize information from two listenings, and analyze ads using this information.

### STEP 1: Organize                                    Suggested Time: 10 minutes

1.  Read the instructions with the class. Have students think about the information they would like to include, checking the audioscript on pages 200–201 if necessary.

2.  Have students complete the chart with information and examples from both listenings. If time allows, have them mingle and compare their information with their classmates'.

3.  Go over the answers with the whole class.

### STEP 2: Synthesize                                   Suggested Time: 15 minutes

1.  Have students work in pairs to discuss the example ads from Listenings One and Two using the questions listed. Emphasize the importance of supporting their statements with examples from Step 1. Move around the room and listen to the discussions.

2.  Invite each pair to share information about at least one ad.

 **Link to NorthStar: Reading and Writing 3**

If students are also using the companion text, you may want to discuss how culture affects the emotional appeals in ads by asking these questions: 1) *Do advertisements in your culture use appeals to emotions? If so, which emotional appeals do you see most often? If not, why not?* 2) *What differences have you noticed between the emotional appeals used in advertising in the United States and in you culture?* To remind students about the cross-cultural aspects of using emotions in advertising, mention how Japanese TV ads manipulate feelings (Reading One: *Advertising All over the World*).

🗀 Go to www.mynorthstarlab.com for *Notetaking* and *Academic Skills Practice*.

# ③ FOCUS ON SPEAKING

## Ⓐ VOCABULARY

### ◀ SKILLS

Review vocabulary from Listenings One and Two; infer meaning of words from context; define new vocabulary; identify parts of speech; use new vocabulary creatively to describe ads.

### ✪ REVIEW                                              Suggested Time: 10 minutes

 Go to www.mynorthstarlab.com for *Review*.

1. Focus students on the target words in the first item of the exercise. Ask them if they can tell you what parts of speech these words are (adjective/noun/ adjective). Explain that this information can be helpful when completing the exercise.

2. Have students complete the exercise individually. Then invite individual students to read their answers to the class.

**Expansion/Homework**
Encourage students to create a vocabulary notebook and organize it according to a variety of criteria (parts of speech, collocations, etc.)

### ✪✪ EXPAND                                             Suggested Time: 15 minutes

1. Have students read the text in **Exercise 1**. Suggest that they read the text all the way to the end first without worrying about new vocabulary items. Then have them read the text again trying to understand the boldfaced words and phrases.

2. Have students complete **Exercise 2** individually or with a partner.

3. Go over the answers with the class and encourage students to give examples to illustrate the meaning of the words.

---

### VOCABULARY EXPANSION: Vocabulary Practice

1. Remind students that they must practice and use vocabulary in order to remember it. Set aside some time each week for students to engage in short, fun practice sessions, adding vocabulary from each unit to recycle and build retention.

2. Use a walk-around strategy to give students an opportunity to practice vocabulary from the first unit. Give half the students an index card with the

*(continued on next page)*

---

vocabulary words. Give the other half an index card with the definitions. Begin the walk around with students exchanging cards when you call stop. On the fourth stop, students should find their match, raise their cards to be checked, and put a sentence on the board if they are correct. Then have students make their own flash cards with words that are still challenging.

## ✪ CREATE

Suggested Time: 20 minutes

1. Place students in small groups and give them a few minutes to review the ads. Be sure they understand what kind of product is being advertised.

2. Have each group discuss the ads using the questions. Remind students to use the vocabulary from the box. Move around the room and listen to the discussions. Provide assistance where necessary. Encourage discussion by asking questions.

3. If time allows, invite groups to share the main points of their discussions. Encourage dissenting views.

 **Link to NorthStar: Reading and Writing 3**
If students are also using the companion text, you may list vocabulary items from Unit 1 of the *Reading and Writing* strand and encourage students to use them in their discussion.

 Go to www.mynorthstarlab.com for additional *Vocabulary* practice.

## ✪✪ B  GRAMMAR: Simple Present and Present Progressive

Go to www.mynorthstarlab.com for *Grammar Chart* and *Exercise 2*.

## ◀ SKILLS

Understand the differences between present simple and present progressive tenses; use the tenses in appropriate contexts.

**Suggested Time: 20 minutes**

1. Have students read the ad in **Exercise 1** silently and then underline and circle examples of each tense. Move around the room and correct students if necessary.

2. Go over the grammar chart with the class. Encourage students to ask questions and invite them to give you examples of each kind of use. Be aware that many languages do not distinguish between simple and progressive tenses, making this a difficult language point for students to comprehend.

3. When you feel students understand the key uses of both tenses, have them work in pairs to complete **Exercise 2**. Go over the answers with the class. Refer back to the grammar explanation if there is uncertainty about an answer.

4. In the same pairs, have students complete **Exercise 3**. Point to the words under each illustration and explain that students should take turns using these words to form sentences describing the pictures.

5. Invite individual students to share a description of an illustration with the entire class. Encourage students to make corrections where appropriate.

**Expansion/Homework**
(1) Choose interesting photographs and have students describe them using the present simple and present progressive. Students can also choose their own from newspapers, magazines, or even personal photographs if they choose. (2) For further practice, offer exercises from *Focus on Grammar 3*, 3rd Edition or Azar's *Fundamentals of English Grammar*, 3rd Edition. See Grammar Book References on page 198 of the student book for specific units and chapters.

 Go to www.mynorthstarlab.com for additional *Grammar* practice.

## C SPEAKING

### SKILLS

Use intonation and stress to emphasize important information; use attention grabbers to get a listener's attention; integrate the concepts, grammar, vocabulary, pronunciation, and function from the unit to create, rehearse, and perform a radio ad.

### PRONUNCIATION: Highlighting

**Suggested Time: 20 minutes**

1. Have students read the information about highlighting. Then play the ad. Next, read the information about stress patterns to the class. Elicit which stress patterns are used in the example ad (pitch, loudness, or length).

2. Have students work with a partner and read the conversation in **Exercise 1**. Encourage them to read the conversation aloud as they circle the highlighted words.

3. Play the conversations and have students check their answers. Go over the answers with the class. Be aware that it can be difficult for many students to distinguish pitch and word length if their languages do not use these strategies for emphasis.

4. Have students work with the same partner to complete **Exercise 2**. Go over the instructions for the exercise to make sure students understand their roles as Student A and B. You may want to demonstrate with a student, making sure to give examples of different stress patterns. Give students 5 minutes to read the ads, circle the highlighted words, and read the text to their partner.

5. Have students switch partners and repeat the exercise.

## ✪✪ FUNCTION: Attention Grabbers

### Suggested Time: 20 minutes

1. Read the explanation of attention grabbers to the class and go over the examples with students.

2. Have students complete **Exercise 1** individually and compare their answers with a partner's. Review the answers with the class.

3. For **Exercise 2**, you may need to write a sample ad before having groups write their own ads. After groups finish, discuss attention grabbers for each product, calling on students to read their attention grabbers to the class. Make sure other students listen to each one carefully so that they can discuss the most interesting attention grabbers.

### Link to *NorthStar: Reading and Writing 3*
If students are also using the companion text, ask them to identify some attention grabbers in Reading Two: *Changing World Markets.* Ask students to discuss how attention grabbers are used in other cultures. Ask them to identify attention grabbers that may work in one culture but not in another.

## ✪✪✪ PRODUCTION: Creating an Advertisement

### Suggested Time: 50 minutes

If you wish to assign a different speaking task than the one in this section, see page 17. The alternative topics relate to the theme of the unit, but may not target the same grammar, pronunciation or function taught in the unit.

1. Explain to students that it is now their turn to use the knowledge they have acquired to create their own radio ad. Read the information in the task box with the class.

2. Go over the instructions for Step 1 with students. Make sure they consider all the points in the instructions. Move around the classroom and listen to the discussions. Provide help where appropriate.

3. Review the instructions for Step 2. Encourage students to write an outline first and then fill in the lines students will say. Monitor progress and make sure all students are participating and target language is being used. Have students go to a corner of the room or into the hallway to practice the ad.

4. Before students present their ads to the class, go over the questions in the Listening Activity, especially the rubric for question 4.

5. Have each group present its ad to the class while the remaining students answer the questions in the Listening Activity.

6. When all ads have been presented, go over the questions in the Listening Activity with the class. Tally the results of question 4 for each ad by a show of hands. Is there a winning ad?

## ✪ ALTERNATIVE SPEAKING TOPICS

These topics give students an alternative opportunity to explore and discuss issues related to the unit theme.

## ✪ RESEARCH TOPICS

**Suggested Time: 30 minutes in class**

1. Have students turn to page 192. Review the instructions for the activity with the class.

2. Show some magazine ads and get students to identify the target audience and techniques used, and evaluate the effectiveness of the ads.

3. Ask students to bring in three magazine ads to class. Divide the class into small groups to discuss the questions. Have each group choose one ad to present to the class.

**Expansion/Homework**
You may want to add a discussion of magazine versus radio advertising. For example, ask: *What kind of products are best suited to each medium? What kinds of appeals are best suited to each?*

 **Link to *NorthStar: Reading and Writing 3***
You may want to ask students to identify the emotional appeals in the billboard advertisements in their community. What emotional appeals is the advertiser using? Why is the advertiser using this appeal to sell the product?

 Go to www.mynorthstarlab.com for *Student Speaking Models, Integrated Task, Video Activity, Internet Activity,* and *Unit 1 Achievement Test.*

# UNIT
# 2 Identity Theft

## OVERVIEW

**Theme:** Fraud

This unit focuses on the topic of identity theft. It explores various ways thieves steal personal information and what steps people can take to detect and prevent identity theft. Students express their opinions and prepare a role play about identity theft prevention.

**Listening One:** *Lily's Story* is a first person narrative describing a woman's experience of being a victim of identity theft.

**Listening Two:** *Public Service Announcements* are announcements on identity theft prevention.

### Critical Thinking

Interpret a photograph
Infer word meaning from context
Classify information
Support opinions with reasons

Choose appropriate punishments for criminal acts
Hypothesize outcomes

### Listening

Predict content
Listen for main ideas
Identify details
Infer implied meaning through intonation

Organize and synthesize information from the listenings
Listen for suggestions to prevent identity theft
Listen for rhythm in speech
Listen to and evaluate student role plays

### Speaking

Express and defend opinions about identity theft
Conduct a role play
Share personal opinions about crime
Agree and disagree with statements

Use strategies for keeping a conversation going
Offer advice for identity theft prevention
Create, practice, and perform a role play

### Vocabulary

Use context clues to find meaning
Determine connotations of words
Use idiomatic expressions
Identify synonyms

### Grammar

Modals of advice

### Pronunciation

Stress in compound words

---

*MyNorthStarLab*
Readiness Check, Background and Vocabulary, Listenings One and Two, Notetaking and Academic Skills Practice, Vocabulary and Grammar, Achievement Test

*NorthStar: Reading and Writing 3*
Unit 2 focuses on the emotional, psychological, and financial consequences of fraud.

Go to www.mynorthstarlab.com for the MyNorthStarLab *Readiness Check*.

# 1 FOCUS ON THE TOPIC

## ◖ SKILLS

Interpret a photograph; share personal knowledge of identity theft; infer the meaning of new vocabulary from context.

## ✪✪✪ Ⓐ PREDICT

**Suggested Time: 5 minutes**

Have students look at the photograph on page 19 and elicit responses to the questions. Ask students to guess what kind of situation the photograph is depicting. Introduce the term *identity theft* and check that students understand the concept.

## ✪✪ Ⓑ SHARE INFORMATION

**Suggested Time: 15 minutes**

1. Invite a student to read the definition of identity theft to the class. Go over any words in the definition that are still unclear.

2. Have students discuss the questions in small groups. Provide some ideas of your own if students are having trouble getting started. Move around the room and ask questions and/or provide support if students have any questions.

3. Invite one student from each group to share the key points of their group's discussion. If time allows, continue the discussion as a whole class.

## ✪✪✪ Ⓒ BACKGROUND AND VOCABULARY

Go to www.mynorthstarlab.com for *Background and Vocabulary*.

**Suggested Time: 25 minutes**

1. Have students look at the title of the article. Ask them if they know what the word *phishing* means. Ask students what word sounds the same. Ask them to tell you what *phishing* and *fishing* have in common. Point to the illustration in the article to help them explain the meaning.

2. Play the recording of the article in **Exercise 1** and have students listen as they read.

3. Have students complete **Exercise 2** in pairs or individually. Then review the answers with the class. Have students point out words or phrases in the article that helped them guess the correct meaning of the words in the exercise.

**Link to *NorthStar: Reading and Writing 3***

If students are also using the companion text, you may want to list vocabulary from Background and Vocabulary, pages 20–21, on the board and see if students can find synonyms for those words in the background passage.

Go to www.mynorthstarlab.com for additional *Background and Vocabulary* practice.

# 2 FOCUS ON LISTENING

## ( SKILLS

Predict the content of a passage; listen for main ideas; identify details; infer information through intonation; express opinions about information in the listening; listen to and discuss Public Service Announcements.

## A LISTENING ONE: Lily's Story

Go to www.mynorthstarlab.com to listen to *Lily's Story*.

**Suggested Time: 5 minutes**

In Listening One, students listen to a woman describe her experiences with identity theft and how it affected her life.

1. Read the introduction with the class. Then play the audio and have students circle the correct answer.

2. Go over the answer with the class. Have students explain their choices.

### LISTENING STRATEGY: Set a Purpose for Listening

1. Discuss why and how we listen. Ask students to brainstorm a list of things we listen to (music, lecture, conversations) and then ask if we listen to all of these in the same way. Write students' ideas on the board.

2. After the list is complete, help students classify the ideas into one of the following categories: to get information, to solve problems, to enjoy, to evaluate. Students might wish to add items as you organize the information. Then have students speculate as to how we might listen differently for each category (for example, information—we might listen more closely to details or we might take notes).

### ✪✪✪ LISTEN FOR MAIN IDEAS

Suggested Time: 10 minutes

1. Play the story without pausing and have students listen and complete the exercise.

2. Go over the answers with the class. Encourage students to correct each other.

### ✪✪✪ LISTEN FOR DETAILS

Suggested Time: 15 minutes

1. Explain to students that they are going to listen to the story again. This time you want them to listen for specific details and use this information to complete the exercise.

2. Play the story again. Have students complete the exercise, circling the correct choices. Invite individual students to read the passage with their selected words and phrases. Encourage other students to call out if they disagree with the choice.

3. If necessary, play the story one more time to give students a chance to review their answers.

---

### REACHING ALL STUDENTS: Listen for Details

- **Less Proficient:** Have students create a web as they listen. Tell them to write any words or phrases they hear during the first listening. Then have small groups discuss and combine information before listening again.

- **More Proficient:** Suggest that students make a web after they listen once. Tell them to put the title in the center and details on each branch of the web.

---

#### Expansion/Homework

This is a good opportunity to talk with students about their strategies for taking notes. You can introduce students to alternatives, such as graphic organizers, or let them share their strategies with the class.

### ✪✪✪ MAKE INFERENCES

Suggested Time: 20 minutes

1. Explain to students that it is possible to convey different meanings depending on intonation of a phrase or sentence. Give a simple example to illustrate this, for example, say *great* once with downward intonation to express displeasure, and once with rising intonation to express enthusiasm.

2. Play the first excerpt for students and go over the intonation markings and meanings as a class. Play the remaining excerpts and have students complete the exercise individually.

3. While students complete the exercise, write the questions and statements from the excerpts on the board. After students complete the exercise, invite individuals to mark the correct intonation on the board. Encourage students to speak up if they disagree. Confirm the implied meaning.

## Expansion/Homework

This exercise is good practice for the TOEFL iBT. You may want to time the questions in order to simulate test conditions. Refer to *NorthStar Building Skills for the TOEFL iBT Intermediate* for more practice for the TOEFL iBT.

## ✪✪✪ EXPRESS OPINIONS                            Suggested Time: 15 minutes

Have students grade each statement individually. Then bring the class together and survey the opinions with a show of hands. Is there any consensus? Invite students to explain their opinions.

### CRITICAL THINKING

Give students the following questions for discussion in small groups before discussing as a whole class:

1. How was Lily's identity stolen?

   Answer: Her wallet was stolen at a restaurant and her information used to obtain credit.

2. Why is this called "identify theft"?

   Answer: The criminal is using the victim's identity and personal information to obtain credit.

3. How do you think you would feel in Lily's situation? Explain.

   Answers might include anger, frustration, fear, insecurity, stress. Students should be able to connect to Lily's feelings, and relate their feelings to clear reasons.

4. What conclusions can you draw from hearing Lily's story?

   Answers will vary, but might include: being careful, reporting theft, and protecting identity. Students should offer reasons to support their answers.

5. How would you solve the problem of identity theft?

   Students can present a variety of logical solutions, but they should give convincing reasons for their choices.

## Expansion/Homework

A good follow up discussion could look at the issue of liability. If a person's identity is stolen, to what extent is this person liable for any purchases made under his or her name? This is a good opportunity to introduce some useful law-related vocabulary.

## ✪✪✪ B   LISTENING TWO: Public Service Announcements

   Go to www.mynorthstarlab.com to listen to *Public Service Announcements*.

**Suggested Time: 10 minutes**

In Listening Two, students listen to two Public Service Announcements that educate the public about identity theft prevention.

1. Read the introduction about PSAs with the class. Explain to students that PSAs are non-commercial advertisements that educate people about important issues such as health or safety. Ask students to give some examples of PSAs they are familiar with.

2. Play the two PSAs and have students check the suggestions they hear. Go over the choices with the class. Then elicit any other suggestions students might have that are not included in the announcements.

## ✪✪✪ C   INTEGRATE LISTENINGS ONE AND TWO

### ◀ SKILLS

Organize information in a chart; synthesize information from the listenings to create a conversation.

**STEP 1: Organize**                          **Suggested Time: 15 minutes**

1. Read the instructions with the class. Have students think about the information they would like to include, checking the audioscript on pages 201–202 if necessary.

2. Have students fill in the chart individually. Then divide the class into pairs and have students compare their answers with a partner's. Move around the room and check answers. Provide help and hints where appropriate.

3. Go over the answers with the whole class.

**STEP 2: Synthesize**                          **Suggested Time: 20 minutes**

1. Explain to students that they will create a short interview between a reporter and police officer about identity theft. Set the scenario for the interview and have each student in the pair choose a role to play.

2. Have students create the interview. Move around and provide support where appropriate. Then have students switch roles and do the interview again. If time allows, invite individual pairs to the front of the class to perform their interviews for their classmates.

   Go to www.mynorthstarlab.com for *Notetaking* and *Academic Skills Practice*.

# ③ FOCUS ON SPEAKING

## Ⓐ VOCABULARY

### ◖ SKILLS

Review vocabulary from Listenings One and Two; determine the connotation of a word; define new idiomatic expressions; identify synonyms; use new vocabulary creatively to talk about identity theft and make suggestions for identity theft prevention.

### ✪ REVIEW                                    Suggested Time: 10 minutes

📁   Go to www.mynorthstarlab.com for *Review*.

1. Explain to the class the meaning of connotation. Have students work in pairs to sort the words in the boxes by connotation.

2. Go over the answers as a class. Encourage discussion. Are there any words that change their connotation through intonation?

**Expansion/Homework**
Introduce the idioms: *glass half full* and *every cloud has a silver lining*. Explain that words and situations can be positive or negative based on a person's perspective. Divide the class into small groups and encourage students to come up with words and/or situations which can be seen from two perspectives. Have each group explain why.

### ✪✪ EXPAND                                   Suggested Time: 15 minutes

1. Have students read the e-mails in **Exercise 1**. Suggest that they read the text all the way to the end first without worrying about new vocabulary items. Then have them read the text again and try to understand the boldfaced phrases.

2. Have students complete **Exercise 2** individually or with a partner.

3. Go over the answers with the class and encourage students to give examples to illustrate the meaning of the words.

---

### VOCABULARY EXPANSION: Phrases

1. Have students create a section for phrases in their personal dictionary. For this unit, have them list the following phrases under a title "Personal Business": *file a complaint, identity theft, proof of identification, credit card*. Students should write an informal definition in their own words and a sentence and illustration which makes the meaning clear.

---

## ✪ CREATE                                              Suggested Time: 20 minutes

1. Go over the questions with the class.

2. Have students work in pairs to brainstorm answers to the questions. Allow them to jot down notes if they wish. Then have students take turns asking and answering questions. Move around the room and listen to the discussions. Ask questions that will elicit the target vocabulary.

 **Link to NorthStar: Reading and Writing 3**
If students are also using the companion text, you might want to list vocabulary items from Unit 2 of the *Reading and Writing* strand and encourage students to use them in their discussions.

Go to www.mynorthstarlab.com for additional *Vocabulary* practice.

## ✪✪ B  GRAMMAR: Modals of Advice

Go to www.mynorthstarlab.com for *Grammar Chart* and *Exercise 2*.

## ◀ SKILLS

Recognize modals of advice and understand their function and correct use; use the appropriate modals to ask for and give advice.

**Suggested Time: 25 minutes**

1. Have students read the cartoon strip in **Exercise 1**. Ask them why they think the mother says, *You should sign it right away.* Explain that the mother is giving her son advice. Write *should* on the board and explain that we use this word to both give and ask for advice.

2. Go over points 1 and 2 in the chart. Elicit some advice from students. For example, ask *What should I do if my credit cards gets stolen?* Be sure to also ask for negative forms, for example, *You shouldn't wait to call the bank and cancel the card.*

3. Go over point 3 with the class. Explain that *had better,* and *had better not* are strong phrases, almost like warnings.

4. Have students complete **Exercise 2** individually. Go over the answers with the class.

5. Divide the class into groups of three and invite one group to the front of the class to read the example for **Exercise 3**. Have students take turns asking for and giving advice. Call on groups to share their pieces of advice with the rest of the class.

**Expansion/Homework**

For further practice, offer exercises from *Focus on Grammar 3*, 3rd Edition or Azar's *Fundamentals of English Grammar*, 3rd Edition. See Grammar Book References on page 198 of the student book for specific units and chapters.

 Go to www.mynorthstarlab.com for additional *Grammar* practice.

## C  SPEAKING

### ◖ SKILLS

Identify and produce correct stress in compound words; use rhetorical devices and intonation to keep a conversation going; integrate the concepts, vocabulary, grammar, pronunciation, and function from the unit to develop a role play.

### ◐◑ PRONUNCIATION: Recognizing Compounds

**Suggested Time: 15 minutes**

1. Explain that compound words can be composed of two or more words, either written together or separately. Elicit some examples from the class.

2. Play Track 19. Have students listen and repeat the words. Ask students if they can find a pattern. Explain that in compound words, the first word has the heaviest stress and high pitch, whether it is made up of two or three and more words.

3. Have students complete **Exercise 1**. Review the answers with the class. Then play Track 20 again and have students repeat the words.

4. Have pairs complete **Exercise 2**. Move around the room and pay attention to pronunciation, especially compounds.

### ◐◑ FUNCTION: Keeping a Conversation Going

**Suggested Time: 20 minutes**

1. Explain to students that in order to keep a conversation going, listeners need to let speakers know they are listening and encourage them to go on speaking. Ask students if they can think of any verbal and non-verbal ways to do this (nodding the head, looking at someone directly in the eyes).

2. Play the conversation in **Exercise 1** and have students underline the words and sounds that help keep the conversation going.

3. Have students look at the chart. Ask individual students to pronounce the words and sounds. Model the intonation if they are having difficulty.

4. Have pairs complete **Exercise 2** using the language from the chart. Move around the room and listen, correcting intonation and pronunciation where appropriate. If time allows, invite two pairs to the front to present their conversations.

## ✪✪✪ PRODUCTION: Role Play

### Suggested Time: 50 minutes

If you wish to assign a different speaking task than the one in this section, see page 34. The alternative topics relate to the theme of the unit, but may not target the same grammar, pronunciation or function taught in the unit.

1. Explain to students that as a final activity, they are going to work in groups of three and create a role play on the topic of identity theft. Go over the information in the task box with the class.

2. Go over Step 1 with the class. Point out that students can choose from the lists in their book or come up with something on their own.

3. Give students 15 minutes to complete Step 1 and allow an additional 15 minutes for each group to practice the role plays. Encourage students to speak as naturally as possible and really "become" the character they have created. Finally, invite each group to perform their role play to the class.

4. **Listening Activity:** Ask the students to watch their classmates' role plays and choose the one they liked best. Have them discuss their choices with a partner.

### Link to *NorthStar: Reading and Writing*
If students are also using the companion text, they might want to use the story of Michelle Brown (Reading Two) as a basis for their role play.

# ✪ ALTERNATIVE SPEAKING TOPICS

These topics give students an alternative opportunity to explore and discuss issues related to the unit theme.

# ✪ RESEARCH TOPICS

**Suggested Time: 30 minutes in class**

1. Have students turn to page 192. Review the instructions for the activity with the class.

2. Have students choose one topic from the box and research it in the library or on the Internet. Encourage students to include additional information they find.

3. Have students present their research findings to the class or in small groups.

 Go to www.mynorthstarlab.com for *Student Speaking Models, Integrated Task, Video Activity, Internet Activity,* and *Unit 2 Achievement Test.*

# Endurance Test

## OVERVIEW

**Theme:** Extreme sports

This unit explores the topic of extreme sports and personal characteristics endurance athletes possess. Students discuss what motivates endurance athletes to participate in extreme sports, and use the information from the unit to analyze and create aphorisms about motivation.

**Listening One:** *Ultrarunner Jay Batchen* is a radio interview with an ultrarunner describing his experience running in the Marathon des Sables in Morocco.

**Listening Two:** *Sports Psychology* is an excerpt from a university lecture on the personal characteristics and motivation of endurance athletes.

### Critical Thinking

Interpret photographs

Rank extreme sports

Infer word meaning from context

Classify information

Support answers with details from the listings

Interpret aphorisms

### Listening

Predict content

Listen for main ideas

Listen for details

Infer speakers' points of view

Organize and synthesize information from the listenings

Classify sounds

### Speaking

Express opinions about extreme sports

Share experiences

Relate personal goals

Conduct an interview

Discuss emotions

Interpret and discuss aphorisms

Create an aphorism

### Vocabulary

Use context clues to find meaning

Define words

Complete a crossword puzzle

### Grammar

Reflexive and reciprocal pronouns

### Pronunciation

Expressions with *other*

*MyNorthStarLab*

Readiness Check, Background and Vocabulary, Listenings One and Two, Notetaking and Academic Skills Practice, Vocabulary and Grammar, Achievement Test

*NorthStar: Reading and Writing 3*

Unit 3 explores the psychological aspects of competitive sports.

Go to www.mynorthstarlab.com for the MyNorthStarLab *Readiness Check*.

# ① FOCUS ON THE TOPIC

### ❰ SKILLS

Predict unit content based on the photograph and unit title; share personal knowledge of extreme sports; infer meaning of new vocabulary from context.

## ✪✪✪ Ⓐ PREDICT

**Suggested Time: 5 minutes**

1. Have students look at the photograph on page 35. Ask students if they can identify the sport and location.

2. Discuss the title of the unit. Be sure students understand the concept of endurance. Have them predict the subject of the unit. Affirm each prediction as a possibility.

## ✪✪ Ⓑ SHARE INFORMATION

**Suggested Time: 15 minutes**

1. Have students look at the photographs of extreme sports. Ask them to list other extreme sports. Write their ideas on the board.

2. Have students in small groups discuss the questions.

3. If time allows, bring the class back together and invite students to share their answers with the class. Encourage discussion.

## ✪✪✪ Ⓒ BACKGROUND AND VOCABULARY

Go to www.mynorthstarlab.com for *Background and Vocabulary*.

**Suggested Time: 25 minutes**

1. Tell students they will read and listen to an article on an extreme sport. Play the recording of the article in **Exercise 1** and have students listen as they read. Explain any unfamiliar vocabulary and have students read and listen again.

2. Have students complete **Exercise 2** in pairs or individually. Then review the answers with the class.

Go to www.mynorthstarlab.com for additional *Background and Vocabulary* practice.

# ②FOCUS ON LISTENING

## ◀ SKILLS

Predict the content of a passage; listen for and correct main ideas; listen for details; infer implied meaning in statements; express opinions about information in the listening; listen to a lecture.

## ✪✪✪ Ⓐ   LISTENING ONE:  Ultrarunner Jay Batchen

📁   Go to www.mynorthstarlab.com to listen to *Ultrarunner Jay Batchen*.

**Suggested Time:  5 minutes**

In Listening One, students hear an interview with a man about his experience as an ultrarunner competing in the Marathon des Sables in Morocco.

1. Play the excerpt. Ask students to think about Jay Batchen's motivation for running in the Marathon des Sables and write their predictions in their books.

2. Have students share their predictions with the class. Affirm each prediction as a possibility.

### LISTENING STRATEGY:  Anticipate Information

1. Tell students that we can improve our listening comprehension by anticipating information we are going to receive as we listen, and a good way to do this is with anticipatory questions.

2. Have students begin by writing the title, *Ultrarunner Jay Batchen,* on the left side of a T-chart, and turning that into a question to get started. Then have students add several *wh-* questions to answer as they listen. They will write the answers to these questions on the right side of the chart.

## ✪✪✪ LISTEN FOR MAIN IDEAS                    Suggested Time:  15 minutes

1. Ask students to read the statements. Play the interview and have students cross out the incorrect statements as they listen. After listening, have students write corrections for each false statement. Play the audio again if necessary to allow students to finish.

2. Have students compare their answers with a partner's. Then invite students to share their answers with the class. Remember that some statements can be corrected in more than one way. Encourage alternative versions.

## ❂❂❂ LISTEN FOR DETAILS Suggested Time: 10 minutes

1. Explain to students that they are going to listen to the interview again. This time you want them to listen for specific details and use this information to circle the best answers.

2. Play the interview again and have students complete the exercise.

3. Go over the answers with the class. If there is any disagreement, replay excerpts from the interview to verify the answers.

### REACHING ALL STUDENTS: Listen for Details

| | |
|---|---|
| • **Less Proficient:** Have students create a character web after listening. Then have them listen a second time to add additional details. | • **More Proficient:** Have students imagine what this competition must be like in terms of the physical challenges and then work with a partner to create a web and a paragraph to describe the race. |

## ❂❂❂ MAKE INFERENCES Suggested Time: 15 minutes

Ask students to pay particular attention to stress and intonation as these are clues to meaning. Then play the excerpts from the interview and have students complete the exercise. Go over the answers with the class.

### Expansion/Homework
If time allows, this is a good opportunity to discuss irony and sarcasm. Certain cultures are very literal and students from these cultures often have difficulty identifying this kind of inferred meaning.

## ❂❂❂ EXPRESS OPINIONS Suggested Time: 15 minutes

1. Have students discuss the questions in small groups. Move around the room and ask questions and provide help where necessary. Encourage students to share personal experiences.

2. Bring the class back together and invite individual students to report on their group discussions. If time allows, continue the discussion as a whole class.

### CRITICAL THINKING

Give students the following questions for discussion in small groups before discussing as a whole class:

1. What makes this race so difficult?

   Answers might vary. Students can cite the length of the race, the terrain, the physical conditions, etc.

**2.** What do you think the runners gain from the experience?

Students can give a variety of answers, but must support them with reasons and/or examples.

**3.** Would you participate in a race like this? Why or why not?

Answers will vary, but students must support their response with clear reasons.

**4.** Why does Jay Batchen say that the race is a *life experience*?

Answers might vary, but students could mention the bond with other racers, the intense physical and emotional challenge, the potential danger—all of which contribute to making this race much more than a race.

---

## ✪✪✪ B  LISTENING TWO: Sports Psychology

📁  Go to www.mynorthstarlab.com to listen to *Sports Psychology*.

**Suggested Time: 10 minutes**

In Listening Two, students listen to an excerpt from a sports psychology lecture. Students gain an understanding of what motivates endurance athletes to practice their sport. They are also given an opportunity to familiarize themselves with the style and language of an academic lecture.

1. Play the excerpt from the university lecture and have students complete the exercise individually.

2. Go over the answers with the class. Replay parts of the lecture if there are disagreements.

**Expansion/Homework**
If time allows, introduce the concepts of intrinsic and extrinsic motivation. What kind of motivation do ultrarunners have? What motivation do the students have to learn English?

---

## ✪✪✪ C  INTEGRATE LISTENINGS ONE AND TWO

### ◀ SKILLS

Organize information from the listenings in a chart; synthesize information from the chart to conduct an interview.

**STEP 1: Organize**                      **Suggested Time: 15 minutes**

1. Focus students on the incomplete chart. Go over the sample answers for question 1. Have students think about the information they would like to include, checking the audioscript on pages 202–203 if necessary.

2. Have students complete the chart with information and examples from both listenings. Then go over the answers with the whole class.

**STEP 2: Synthesize**                              **Suggested Time: 20 minutes**

1. Have students work with a partner. Have them compare their charts and add detail where appropriate.

2. Set up the interview. Be sure students understand the two roles. Have Student A ask the questions to Student B and then switch roles and repeat the conversation a second time.

3. If time allows, invite pairs to present their interviews to the rest of the class.

Go to www.mynorthstarlab.com for *Notetaking* and *Academic Skills Practice*.

# ③ FOCUS ON SPEAKING

## A VOCABULARY

### ◖ SKILLS

Review vocabulary from Listenings One and Two; apply vocabulary learned in the unit to a new context—a crossword puzzle; match idioms with their definitions; reflect on personal goals using vocabulary from the unit.

### ✪ REVIEW                              **Suggested Time: 15 minutes**

1. Show students the crossword puzzle. Be sure they understand the concept. Then focus students on the list of words and explain that they must use these words to complete the clue sentences and then write the words in the correct place in the crossword puzzle.

2. Have students work on the puzzle independently for 10 minutes and then compare their answers with a partner's.

3. Go over the answers with the class. If you have an overhead projector or interactive whiteboard, project the crossword puzzle on the screen. Fill in the puzzle as you go over the answers with the class.

**Expansion/Homework**
You can turn this exercise into a game. Divide the class into small groups to complete the puzzle. Award a prize to the group that finishes first.

## ✪✪ EXPAND

📁 Go to www.mynorthstarlab.com for *Expand*.

1. Play the conversation in **Exercise 1** while students read the transcript.

2. Have students complete **Exercise 2**. Go over the answers as a class.

### Expansion/Homework

Ask students if they have any idioms in their own language to express similar ideas. Have students translate them and share them with the class. Are their idioms the same as the English ones? Are there any similarities between students' native languages?

---

### VOCABULARY EXPANSION: Words with Multiple Meanings

1. Remind students that one of the challenges of learning English are words that have multiple meanings. Give students an example of a word with several meanings in context (for example, *While he waited for them to* <u>roll</u> *the sacks of sugar into the bakery, he ate a* <u>roll</u> *and watched them* <u>roll</u> *the dough for the pies*).

2. Write these words on the board: *course, stage, sand, ration,* and *goal*. Have students work in groups to look up meanings and choose the one that fits the use in the interview. Then have the groups draw illustrations to show the different meanings for each word on large chart paper to present to the class.

---

## ✪ CREATE

1. Go over the instructions in **Exercise 1**. Initiate a discussion of goals by creating a mind map with the word *goals* in a circle at its center. Invite students to share their goals and add them to the mind map along with the examples from the student book.

2. Review the vocabulary in the box and go over the questions in **Exercise 2**. Pay special attention to questions 4 and 6, which can be hard to understand, and may be uncomfortable issues for students to discuss.

3. Move around the room and help students where appropriate. Ask questions to draw out concrete examples from students.

4. If time allows, invite pairs to share their discussion of goals with the rest of the class. Do not have students share their own goals, but have partners describe each other's experiences.

 **Link to *NorthStar: Reading and Writing 3***

If students are also using the companion text, you may list vocabulary items from Unit 3 of the *Reading and Writing* strand and encourage students to use them in their discussion.

📁 Go to www.mynorthstarlab.com for additional *Vocabulary* practice.

## ✦✦ Ⓑ GRAMMAR: Reflexive and Reciprocal Pronouns

📁 Go to www.mynorthstarlab.com for *Grammar Chart* and *Exercise 2.*

### ◖ SKILLS

Understand the use of reflexive and reciprocal pronouns and their relationship to the subject of a sentence.

**Suggested Time: 20 minutes**

1. Read the excerpt from the article on motivation in **Exercise 1** with the class. Ask students to identify the reflexive and reciprocal pronouns and draw a line from pronoun to the subject it refers to.

2. Go over point 1 in the grammar chart with the class. If time allows, call out various subjects (for example, the president, Tony and Jim, etc.) and have students call out the correct reflexive pronouns.

3. Review points 2 and 3. Make sure students understand the distinction between reciprocal and reflexive pronouns. Pay special attention to point 4 and how choice of pronouns changes meaning.

4. Have students complete **Exercise 2** individually. Go over the answers with the class.

5. Have students work in pairs to complete **Exercise 3**. Go over the example before they start. Move around the room and listen to discussions.

6. Bring the class together and invite students to share their answers. Remember that there is more than one answer to each question, so encourage students to present alternatives.

### Expansion/Homework

(**1**) You can assign **Exercise 2** as homework. Have students check answers in the Answer Key or go over the answers as a class. (**2**) For further practice, offer exercises from *Focus on Grammar 3,* 3rd Edition or Azar's *Fundamentals of English Grammar,* 3rd Edition. See Grammar Book References on page 198 of the student book for specific units and chapters.

📁 Go to www.mynorthstarlab.com for additional *Grammar* practice.

## Ⓒ SPEAKING

### ◖ SKILLS

Recognize and practice the pronunciation of *other* when joined with other words; express and ask for an opinion; integrate the concepts, vocabulary, grammar, pronunciation, and function from the unit to explain and create aphorisms.

## ✪✪ PRONUNCIATION: Expressions with *other*

**Suggested Time: 20 minutes**

1. Write the word *other* on the board and elicit expressions that contain this word. Play Track 31 and ask students to pay attention to the pronunciation of the boldfaced phrases. See if students can identify any pronunciation patterns, then go over the pronunciation points in the chart.

2. Play the audio in **Exercise 1** and have students listen and repeat what they hear. Then have them choose three of the phrases to say to the class. If your class is large, you can do this step as pair work and then ask a couple of students to say their phrases to the class.

3. Have students complete **Exercise 2** and compare their answers with a partner's. Go over the answers as a class.

4. In pairs, have students match Student A's part and Student B's part in **Exercise 3** to create logical mini-conversations. Invite pairs to repeat the conversations in front of the class and elicit the meaning of the underlined idioms.

## ✪✪ FUNCTION: Expressing and Asking for Opinions

**Suggested Time: 20 minutes**

1. Call on three students to read the conversation in **Exercise 1** for the class. Then go over the information in the chart and answer any questions.

2. Have students complete **Exercise 2**. Go over the answers with the class. If there is any disagreement about the answers, refer students to the chart.

3. Have students study the photographs in **Exercise 3**. Elicit words describing emotions and write a few of them on the board.

4. Have students work in small groups to interpret the athletes' feelings in the pictures. Encourage discussion and diverging opinions.

5. If time allows, invite groups to share their interpretations and discuss them with the rest of the class.

## ✪✪✪ PRODUCTION: Small Group Discussion

**Suggested Time: 50 minutes**

If you wish to assign a different speaking task than the one in this section, see page 52. The alternative topics relate to the theme of the unit, but may not target the same grammar, pronunciation or function taught in the unit.

1. Read the information in the task box with the class. Go over the definition of *aphorism* carefully to make sure students understand the concept. Elicit any aphorisms the students may already know in English. Take care to distinguish between aphorisms and idioms. This can be confusing for students.

2. Explain the steps in the exercise and then divide the class into small groups. This is a difficult activity for students. Move around the room and help groups focus their discussion on specific, concrete situations related to motivation.

3. Have students write the aphorisms on large pieces of paper and hang them up around the classroom. Allow students to wander through the "aphorism gallery" and think about the meanings.

4. Invite each group to present their aphorism and explain its meaning to the class.

 **Link to *NorthStar: Reading and Writing 3***
If students are also using the companion text, encourage them to use the interview with Tony Hawk (Reading One) for ideas.

---

## ✪ ALTERNATIVE SPEAKING TOPICS

These topics give students an alternative opportunity to explore and discuss issues related to the unit theme.

---

## ✪ RESEARCH TOPICS

**Suggested Time: 30 minutes in class**

1. Have students turn to page 193. Review the instructions for the activity with the class, and give some general guidelines for the short presentation.

2. Have students choose one sport from the box and research it in the library or on the Internet. Emphasize that students' research should include answers to the questions listed in the book. Encourage students to include additional information they find. Remind students to bring at least one picture of the sport. Tell students they can create posters about the sport to display in the classroom.

3. Have students present their research findings (and their posters) to the class or in small groups.

Go to www.mynorthstarlab.com for *Student Speaking Models, Integrated Task, Video Activity, Internet Activity,* and *Unit 3 Achievement Test.*

# Sprtd by the Same Language

## OVERVIEW

**Theme:** Language
This unit explores the topic of language dialects. It explains various dialects and examines how dialect affects our sense of identity. Students are encouraged to think about dialect and identity and to share their opinions on the topic.

**Listening One:** *Accent and Identity* is an interview, in which a student describes his experience speaking a West Indies dialect in the United States.

**Listening Two:** *Code-Switching* is an excerpt from a lecture on code-switching and teenage slang.

### Critical Thinking

Interpret a cartoon
Identify accents
Recognize personal bias towards accents
Infer word meaning from context

Read a map
Hypothesize scenarios
Analyze problems and propose solutions
Hypothesize another's point of view

### Listening

Predict content
Listen for main ideas and details
Listen closely to interpret a speaker's emotions
Infer attitudes on accents from statements

Take notes on a lecture
Identify opinions about accents
Organize and synthesize information from the
    listenings

### Speaking

Express and defend opinions about accents
Conduct an interview
Play a game of *Truth or Dare*

Present a plan to improve English skills
Lead a group discussion
Discuss solutions to a problem

### Vocabulary

Use context clues to find meaning
Use idiomatic expressions

### Grammar

Modals of ability and possibility

### Pronunciation

*Can / Can't*

**MyNorthStarLab**
Readiness Check, Background and
Vocabulary, Listenings One and Two,
Notetaking and Academic Skills Practice,
Vocabulary and Grammar, Achievement Test

**NorthStar: Reading and Writing 3**
Unit 4 focuses on language and gender
and the discussion of how gender
determines the way we use language.

# ①FOCUS ON THE TOPIC

## ◖SKILLS

Predict content based on a cartoon and unit title; recognize and discuss differences in accents; reflect on personal bias towards accents; infer the meaning of new vocabulary from context.

## ✦✦✦Ⓐ PREDICT

**Suggested Time: 10 minutes**

1. Have students read the cartoon on page 53. Read the cartoon aloud, simulating the accents, if you can.

2. Discuss the questions with the class. Ask students if there are similar dialectal differences among speakers of their native language.

## ✦✦Ⓑ SHARE INFORMATION

**Suggested Time: 15 minutes**

1. Ask students to check the items individually. If you have a multinational classroom, create groups of mixed nationality and have students compare and discuss their lists. It is also interesting to have students from the same language group compare their lists and see if they agree.

2. Ask a student from each group to summarize their group's discussion. Write the main points on the board.

3. Have a whole class discussion about question 2. Try and focus on the features that "better" dialects have in common.

⟳ **Link to *NorthStar: Reading and Writing 3***
If students are also using the companion text, you can ask them to discuss how gender affects accent or speaking style. Some possible questions include: *Do men and women have different ways of speaking? If so, what are they? Do you think there are certain words that only men or women use? What are they?*

📁 Go to www.mynorthstarlab.com for *Background and Vocabulary*.

**Suggested Time: 25 minutes**

1. Tell students they will read and listen to an excerpt from a linguistics textbook about dialects. Play the recording of the text in **Exercise 1** and have students listen as they read. Tell students to pay attention to the boldfaced words and phrases and to underline any unfamiliar vocabulary.

2. Have students read the article again if necessary. Go over the vocabulary students underlined and explain the meaning.

3. Have students complete **Exercise 2** in pairs or individually. Then review the answers with the class.

**Expansion/Homework**

If time allows, encourage students to share any anecdotes they know similar to the case studies.

📁 Go to www.mynorthstarlab.com for additional *Background and Vocabulary* practice.

# FOCUS ON LISTENING

## ◖ SKILLS

Recognize English accents; listen for main ideas; listen for details; infer emotions and attitudes on accents from statements; express opinions about accents and identity; listen to a lecture.

★★★ A **LISTENING ONE: Accent and Identity**

📁 Go to www.mynorthstarlab.com to listen to *Accent and Identity*.

**Suggested Time: 5 minutes**

In Listening One, students hear an interview between two graduate students discussing one student's experience speaking a West Indies dialect in the United States.

1. Point to the map. Ask students what the identified countries have in common (English as an official language).

2. Play the excerpt from the interview and see if students can identify Peter's accent.

## LISTENING STRATEGY: Determine Speaker's Purpose

1. Remind students that, just as we have a specific purpose for listening, a speaker has a purpose for speaking. They might speak to inform, to entertain, or to persuade.

2. Go back to Units 1–3 and have students work in small groups to determine the purpose for each of the speakers. First, they can decide on a simple, one-two word purpose (for example, to inform), and then expand that to a sentence (The speaker gives information about ...).

### ✪✪✪ LISTEN FOR MAIN IDEAS                   Suggested Time: 10 minutes

1. Play the interview without pausing and have students complete the exercise. Play the audio again if necessary to allow students to finish.

2. Go over the answers with the class.

### ✪✪✪ LISTEN FOR DETAILS                      Suggested Time: 15 minutes

1. Explain to students that they are going to listen to the interview again. This time you want them to listen for specific details and use this information to complete the sentences in the exercise. Play the interview again. Have students listen and circle the best answers.

2. Go over the answers with the class. If there is any disagreement, replay excerpts from the interview to verify the answers.

### ✪✪✪ MAKE INFERENCES                         Suggested Time: 15 minutes

1. Go over the instructions with the class. Tell students they will need to identify Peter's feelings and attitudes toward his accent based on what he says.

2. Play the excerpts. Stop between each excerpt to give students enough time to write their answers.

3. Invite students to share their answers with the class and open up the subject to discussion. Emphasize that since it is an inference exercise, there is not one correct answer to each question.

## REACHING ALL STUDENTS: Make Inferences

- **Less Proficient:** Provide audioscripts and have student partners assume the roles of Peter and Lisa to read each excerpt before they listen and answer inference questions.

- **More Proficient:** Have students extend the interview with Peter and Lisa, adding a cultural issue that new students have to deal with (clothes, food, music, etc.). Have them write an excerpt that defines and shows a solution to the issue.

## ✪✪✪ EXPRESS OPINIONS

**Suggested Time: 15 minutes**

1. Have students discuss the questions in small groups. Move around the room and ask additional questions and/or provide help where necessary. Encourage students to share personal experiences.

2. Bring the class back together and invite individual students to report on their group discussions. If time allows, continue the discussion as a class.

---

### CRITICAL THINKING

Give students the following questions for discussion in small groups before discussing as a whole class:

1. How did Peter attempt to solve the problem of not fitting in?

   Answer: He worked to change his accent.

2. How does he feel about his accent now? Why?

   Answer: He feels comfortable with it because he sees it as part of his identity.

3. How do you feel about your accent? Explain.

   Students will offer different information, but should be able to provide an explanation to support their feelings.

4. What advice would you give a new student about his/her language and accent? Explain.

   Students will give a variety of responses which should be supported by reasons and examples.

---

### Expansion/Homework

Have students discuss the concept of English as an international language. What happens to dialects when English is used by two non-native speakers of English?

---

## ✪✪✪ **B** LISTENING TWO: Code-Switching

Go to www.mynorthstarlab.com to listen to *Code-Switching*.

**Suggested Time: 10 minutes**

Listening Two is an excerpt from a university lecture on code-switching. Students learn about teenage slang as an example of code-switching. The listening gives students the opportunity to familiarize themselves with the style and language of a university lecture and practice academic notetaking.

1. Have students look at the lecture notes. Read over the introductory explanation and the definition of code.

2. Play the lecture and have students complete the notes. Go over the answers as a class. Replay segments if some points remain unclear.

### Expansion/Homework

Invite students to share alternative examples of notetaking they might use.

◖ **SKILLS**

Organize information from the listenings in a chart; synthesize information from the chart to conduct an interview.

### STEP 1: Organize                                    Suggested Time: 15 minutes

1. Read the instructions with the class. Have students think about the information they would like to include, checking the audioscript on pages 203–204 if necessary.

2. Have students choose the correct opinions and cite examples from the lecture to support their answers.

3. Go over the answers with the whole class. If there is disagreement, encourage students to point to the information in the listenings that supports their answers.

### STEP 2: Synthesize                                   Suggested Time: 20 minutes

1. Divide the class into groups of three. Have students choose what roles they want to play.

2. Have students practice their interviews. Then have them switch roles and repeat the conversation two more times so that all students have a chance to play each role. Move around the room and assist students if necessary.

3. If time allows, invite a few groups to present their interviews to the rest of the class.

     Go to www.mynorthstarlab.com for *Notetaking* and *Academic Skills Practice*.

# ③ FOCUS ON SPEAKING

## **A** VOCABULARY

◖ **SKILLS**

Review vocabulary from Listenings One and Two; infer meaning of words from context; expand vocabulary by defining new idiomatic expressions; use new vocabulary creatively in real communication.

## ✪ REVIEW

📁 Go to www.mynorthstarlab.com for *Review*.

1. Go over the example quote with the class. Have students work in pairs to complete the exercise.

2. Call on individual students to read the completed quotes.

## ✪✪ EXPAND
**Suggested Time: 10 minutes**

1. Play the conversation in **Exercise 1** while students listen and read the transcript. Go over the boldfaced phrases with students and have them attempt to explain the meaning of each phrase.

2. Have students complete **Exercise 2**. Go over the answers as a class. Make sure students understand the meaning of the idioms.

---

### VOCABULARY EXPANSION: Vocabulary Picture

1. Have students draw a bold outline of an object (for example, car, map, tree) that will fit the concept they are studying or reading about. They can overlay a blank page so that the outline shows through. Then they select 5–8 related vocabulary words and write the words and definitions to create the outline of the picture/object selected.

2. Students might draw a map of St. Vincent, a person, or lips. Then they would choose vocabulary words appropriate to their choice. If they outlined lips or mouth, for example, they might choose *accents, identity, dialect, self-conscious, slang,* and *comment on* to make their vocabulary picture.

---

## ✪ CREATE
**Suggested Time: 25 minutes**

1. Go over the rules of the game *Truth or Dare*. This game might be unfamiliar to many students. Read through the instructions, making sure that students understand each step. You might want to demonstrate the steps of the game with a student.

2. Place students in groups of five or six and give each student a pair of dice or twelve pieces of paper numbered 1–12.

3. Move around the room and verify that students are playing the game correctly. Monitor use of target vocabulary and ensure that answers are not insulting or offensive to other students. Keep the game light and positive.

 **Link to *NorthStar: Reading and Writing 3***
If students are also using the companion text, you can have them select vocabulary from Unit 4 of the *Reading and Writing* strand and use it to write more *Truth or Dare* questions.

📁 Go to www.mynorthstarlab.com for additional *Vocabulary* practice.

## B GRAMMAR: Modals of Ability and Possibility

Go to www.mynorthstarlab.com for *Grammar Chart* and *Exercise 1*.

### SKILLS

Understand and practice the use of modals of ability and possibility and use them to discuss past experiences and future possibility.

**Suggested Time: 25 minutes**

1. Have students read the paragraph in **Exercise 1** and underline the target modals. Discuss the follow-up questions with the class.
2. Go over the information and the examples in the chart. Make sure students understand the difference between *can* and *could.*
3. Have students work in pairs to complete **Exercise 2**. If possible, pair students from different language backgrounds.
4. Have students write answers to the question in **Exercise 3** individually and then share their lists with a classmate. If possible, do a mix-and-mingle exercise, and have students walk around the classroom sharing their lists with other classmates.

**Expansion/Homework**

For further practice, offer exercises from *Focus on Grammar 3,* 3rd Edition or Azar's *Fundamentals of English Grammar,* 3rd Edition. See Grammar Book References on page 198 of the student book for specific units and chapters.

Go to www.mynorthstarlab.com for additional *Grammar* practice.

## C SPEAKING

### SKILLS

Distinguish between and practice the pronunciation of *can* and *can't;* lead a discussion; express and defend opinions; integrate the concepts, vocabulary, grammar, pronunciation, and function from the unit to analyze a problem and propose solutions.

### PRONUNCIATION: *Can/Can't*

**Suggested Time: 15 minutes**

1. Go over the explanation with the class and play the example conversation. See if students can identify the difference in pronunciation between *can* and *can't.*

2. Review the pronunciation chart with the class. Have students practice the pronunciation of *can* and *can't* individually.

3. Have students complete **Exercise 1** individually and then compare their answers with a partner's. Then review the answers as a class.

4. Read the instructions for **Exercise 2**. Have students complete the exercise with a partner. Move around the classroom and monitor pronunciation of *can* and *can't*.

**Expansion/Homework**

You can provide more practice by having students participate in a chain drill. Divide the class into small groups (preferably in a circle). The first student begins by saying a sentence with *can* and *can't*. For example, *I can speak Russian, but I can't speak Chinese.* The next student repeats what the first student says and adds another sentence of his/her own. For example, *He can speak Russian, but he can't speak Chinese. I can speak Tagalog, but I can't speak French.* The sentences do not need to be related to languages as long as students use *can* and *can't*. For example, *I can ride a skateboard, but I can't ski.*

## ✪✪ FUNCTION: Leading a Small Group Discussion

**Suggested Time: 25 minutes**

1. Have students look at the pictures in **Exercise 1** and match the parts of a discussion to the appropriate pictures. Then invite a student to read aloud the short paragraph on leading a group discussion.

2. Place students in small groups of four. Have them read the phrases for discussion in **Exercise 2**, brainstorm additional phrases, and write them in the blanks.

3. Introduce the topic of improving one's pronunciation. Point out the pronunciation activities in the box in **Exercise 3**. One student from each group will lead the discussion while the other three discuss the topic using examples from the box or their own ideas. Repeat the activity so that each student gets a chance to play all roles.

## ✪✪✪ PRODUCTION: Leading a Small Group Discussion

**Suggested Time: 50 minutes**

If you wish to assign a different speaking task than the one in this section, see page 72. The alternative topics relate to the theme of the unit, but may not target the same grammar, pronunciation or function taught in the unit.

1. Have one student read the information in the task box to the class. Tell students they will prepare a discussion about language. Next, read the situations with the class and make sure students understand each one. You may want to point out that a Mississippi accent is often stereotyped as being uneducated.

2. Divide the class into groups of four. Have each student choose a different situation. Starting with Situation 1, have each student lead a discussion.

3. Move around the room and monitor the discussions. Keep the students on topic. Encourage them to use phrases and vocabulary from the unit. Point out the uses of *could,* to describe future possibility, and *should,* which describes advice.

4. Bring the class together and ask each group to share their solutions to the four situations. Encourage students to ask their classmates questions and query their solutions.

### Expansion/Homework
Use the situations as the basis for a role play activity. Students can work in pairs to create the role play using phrases and vocabulary from the unit. They can also write a short summary of their discussions for homework.

### Link to *NorthStar: Reading and Writing 3*
If students are also using the companion text, you may want to suggest an additional situation as a basis for discussion and/or role play: *Monica is the only female manager in her company. She feels frustrated because the other managers, who are male, don't seem to take her seriously. Also, she doesn't like the way the other managers talk to each other because it seems rude. She is worried that she won't be able to fit in.*

## ✪ ALTERNATIVE SPEAKING TOPICS

These topics give students an alternative opportunity to explore and discuss issues related to the unit theme.

## ✪ RESEARCH TOPICS

**Suggested Time: 30 minutes in class**

1. Have students turn to page 193. Review the instructions for the activity with the class. Help students identify people that they can interview. Make sure students understand that slang refers to informal, youth-oriented speech while jargon refers to technical speech within a professional field.

2. Have students conduct their research. Encourage them to use the Internet for additional information.

3. Have students report back to the class or in small groups by writing the slang or jargon words on the board or piece of paper and having their classmates guess their meaning before explaining them to the class or group.

 Go to www.mynorthstarlab.com for *Student Speaking Models, Integrated Task, Video Activity, Internet Activity,* and *Unit 4 Achievement Test.*

# Culture and Commerce

## OVERVIEW

**Theme:** Tourism

This unit focuses on the positive and negative aspects of tourism. Students explore the topic of the effects of tourism on culture and economy, and discuss advantages and disadvantages of tourism. They also collaborate to reach a compromise on a controversial topic related to tourism.

**Listening One:** *Tourist Attraction or Human Zoo?* is a news report discussing travel to the Pa Daung region of Thailand, which is known for its long-necked women.

**Listening Two:** *Town Hall Meeting in Cape Cod* is an excerpt from a town hall meeting in which participants are discussing the impact of tourism on their region.

### Critical Thinking

Interpret a photograph
Infer word meaning from context
Evaluate advantages and disadvantages
Support opinions with reasons

Classify information
Read a map
Hypothesize outcomes
Collaborate to reach a compromise

### Listening

Predict content
Listen for main ideas and details
Infer speakers' emotions
Identify contrasting viewpoints in the listening

Organize and synthesize information from the listenings
Categorize sounds

### Speaking

Agree and disagree with statements
Discuss the pros and cons of tourism
Talk about a tourist destination

Hypothesize possible outcomes
Make suggestions
Participate in a simulation

### Vocabulary

Use context clues to find meaning
Define words
Group words with similar meaning
Use idiomatic expressions

### Grammar

Future predictions with *if*-clauses

### Pronunciation

Words spelled with *o*

📁 **MyNorthStarLab**
Readiness Check, Background and Vocabulary, Listenings One and Two, Notetaking and Academic Skills Practice, Vocabulary and Grammar, Achievement Test

📚 **NorthStar: Reading and Writing 3**
Unit 5 focuses on the topic of ecotourism.

# FOCUS ON THE TOPIC

## ◀ SKILLS

Interpret a photograph; express opinions about tourism; infer meaning of new vocabulary from context.

## ✪✪✪ **A** PREDICT

**Suggested Time: 5 minutes**

1.  Have students look at the picture of the long-necked women. Ask the class: *Why do you think these women are wearing coils around their necks?*

2.  Point to the title of the unit. Elicit the meaning of the word *commerce* or explain it to the class.

3.  In pairs, have students discuss the relationship between culture and commerce in tourism. Invite a few pairs to share their ideas with the class.

## ✪✪ **B** SHARE INFORMATION

**Suggested Time: 15 minutes**

1.  Explain to students that you want to get their opinion on statements related to tourism. Have students read the questions silently and ask them if they have any vocabulary questions.

2.  Read the first statement with the class. Ask student opinions by a show of hands. Be sure students are clear about the degree of agreement and disagreement each statement implies. Have students complete the remaining statements individually.

3.  Divide the class into small groups (preferably with a mix of fluency levels) and have students discuss their answers.

4.  If time allows, ask one student from each group to summarize their discussions to the class.

**Expansion/Homework**
You can use the statement in this exercise in a debate. Divide the class into two groups—a pro group and a con group. Choose one or two statements from the exercise and have groups conduct a debate.

## ✸✸✸ Ⓒ BACKGROUND AND VOCABULARY

📁 Go to www.mynorthstarlab.com for *Background and Vocabulary*.

**Suggested Time: 20 minutes**

1. Ask students if they know what a blog is. Explain that a blog is a web log: a journal on the Internet. See if students can think of any other blogs they might know. Maybe they have their own blog? Explain that many people share their experiences in a blog. The blog they will read and listen to describes a visit to Thailand.

2. Play the recording of the blog in **Exercise 1** and have students listen as they read.

3. Have students complete **Exercise 2**, matching the boldfaced words with the correct definition.

4. Go over the answers with the class. Take this opportunity to expand on the definitions and encourage students to personalize meaning with concrete examples.

**Expansion/Homework**
Ask students to read a blog on the web. Have them share the blog (including the URL) with the class.

◯◯◯ **Link to NorthStar: Reading and Writing 3**
If students are also using the companion text, you can have them write a short blog about traveling to Antarctica.

📁 Go to www.mynorthstarlab.com for additional *Background and Vocabulary* practice.

# ②FOCUS ON LISTENING

## ◖SKILLS

Make predictions about the content of the story; listen for main ideas; listen for details; make inferences about people's feelings based on tone of voice; agree and disagree with statements about Pa Daung women; express and defend opinions about Pa Daung women; listen to an excerpt from a meeting.

## ✸✸✸ Ⓐ LISTENING ONE: Tourist Attraction or Human Zoo?

📁 Go to www.mynorthstarlab.com to listen to *Tourist Attraction or Human Zoo?*

**Suggested Time: 5 minutes**

Listening One is a radio report on travel to the Pa Daung region of Thailand, which is known for its long-necked women. It presents a balanced description of the effect of tourism on the region through the opinions of four interviewees.

1. Explain to students that they will hear an excerpt from a news report. The students must listen and then choose which answer best represents the way the speaker presents the topic.

2. Have students listen and then invite volunteers to share their answers. Ask them for examples from the listening to support their position.

## LISTENING STRATEGY: Create a Listening Guide

To help students focus on the content of a speaker's message, have students create a generic listening guide similar to the following:

| | |
|---|---|
| Name of speaker: | Date: |
| Title/Subject: | Genre/Form: |
| Purpose for Listening: | Speaker's Purpose: |
| People: | |
| Places: | |
| Ideas: | |

### ✪✪✪ LISTEN FOR MAIN IDEAS                    Suggested Time: 15 minutes

1. Read the instructions with the class. Tell students to listen and decide whether the statements are true or false based on the information in the listening.

2. Play the news report once and have students complete the exercise.

3. Review the answers together with the class. If there are any disagreements, you can play the audio one more time.

### ✪✪✪ LISTEN FOR DETAILS                    Suggested Time: 15 minutes

1. Explain to students that they are going to listen to the news report again. This time you want them to listen for specific details and use this information to complete the sentences in the exercise.

2. Play the news report again and have students complete the exercise individually.

3. Call on individual students for answers. If there are any disagreements, you can replay the relevant segments or play the whole report one more time.

### ✪✪✪ MAKE INFERENCES                    Suggested Time: 15 minutes

1. Review the adjectives in the box. Make sure students understand what they mean. Invite students to try and say a sentence or two in various tones of voice, for example, frustrated, confident, accepting. See if the other students can guess what tone of voice they are using.

2. Read the instructions with the class. Play Excerpt One and work through the example with the class. Play the remaining excerpts and have students fill in the blanks.

3. Review the answers with the class. Allow for varying opinions and encourage discussion. Replay the excerpts if necessary. As you discuss answers, emphasize that students are welcome to express varying opinions as long as their reasoning is sound.

## REACHING ALL STUDENTS: Make Inferences

- **Less Proficient:** Before assigning inference questions, demonstrate how feelings can be inferred from tone of voice.

- **More Proficient:** Suggest that students write a short explanation for each answer, using information from the listening and from their own knowledge.

## ✪✪✪ EXPRESS OPINIONS                              Suggested Time: 15 minutes

1. Read the two statements about the Pa Daung tribe to the class.

2. Have students work in small groups to discuss their opinions about the statements. Have one student take notes on what is said.

3. Invite one student from each group to summarize their discussion to the rest of the class.

4. Ask students to write key points they make on the board.

**Link to *NorthStar: Reading and Writing 3***
If students are also using the companion text, you can ask them to compare traveling to the Pa Daung region to traveling to Antarctica. Focus on the topic of impact of tourism on each region.

## CRITICAL THINKING

Give students the following questions for discussion in small groups before discussing as a whole class:

1. How do the Myanmar women earn money for their families?

   Answer: They pose for photos, sell souvenirs, and talk with tourists.

2. Why do they stretch their necks?

   Answer: It was once a tradition, but now is a means to earn money.

3. Which position do you agree with: tourists are supporting their tradition or tourists are treating them like animals in a zoo? Explain.

   Students will choose either position, but must offer specific reasons and examples to support their opinion.

*(continued on next page)*

**4.** Compare the neck rings to other methods that people use to alter their bodies.

Several comparisons can be made (tattoos, implants, piercings, foot binding). Encourage students to explore those comparisons in terms of harm to the body, pain and inconvenience, irreversible decisions, or attractiveness, tradition, and lifestyle.

## ❊❊❊ B LISTENING TWO: Town Hall Meeting in Cape Cod

Go to www.mynorthstarlab.com to listen to *Town Hall Meeting in Cape Cod.*

**Suggested Time: 15 minutes**

Listening Two is an excerpt from a town hall meeting in Cape Cod, at which residents express their opinions about the effects of tourism in their area. The purpose of the listening is to broaden students' understanding of the positive and negative aspects of tourism.

1. Ask students to look at the maps and related article in **Exercise 1**. See if students are familiar with Cape Cod. Ask students to discuss possible reasons why Cape Cod is attractive to tourists. Ask students to give examples of other similar destinations.

2. Write the term *town hall meeting* on the board. Elicit what a town hall meeting is. Discuss briefly who might attend a town meeting and why.

3. Play the audio and have students complete **Exercise 2**. Review answers as a class.

**Expansion/Homework**

Have students brainstorm other controversial issues that might affect a town. Invite one or two pairs to come to the front of the class and present both sides of each issue.

## ❊❊❊ C INTEGRATE LISTENINGS ONE AND TWO

### ◀ SKILLS

Organize information from the listenings by reviewing the positive and negative aspects of tourism; synthesize information from the listenings to discuss the pros and cons of tourism; agree and disagree with statements.

### STEP 1: Organize                    Suggested Time: 10 minutes

1. Have students work with a partner. Tell students they will need to use information from both listenings to complete the chart.

2. Draw a simple copy of the chart on the board and write the example in the appropriate box. If necessary, trace your fingers from left to right and top to bottom until they meet in the upper right quadrant.

3. Have pairs complete their charts. Call on individual students to write their answers in the chart on the board. Then call on students to identify effects shared by both communities and circle them in the chart.

## STEP 2: Synthesize                                    Suggested Time: 20 minutes

1. Read the instructions with the class. Explain that one student in the pair will argue the pro position and the other will take the con position. Explain to students that they need not really share the position they are defending. Rather, they should make the best argument possible based on the information they generated with their partner.

2. Before the discussions begin, briefly note the Useful Language cited in the Student Book. Elicit some example sentences or provide some of your own.

3. Move around the room and listen to the discussions. Encourage use of the new vocabulary from the unit. Offer assistance where necessary.

4. Invite students to share some of the points of their discussion with the rest of the class.

 **Link to** *NorthStar: Reading and Writing 3*
(1) If students are also using the companion text, refer them to the grammar point on page 91 of the *Reading and Writing* strand (*because* and *even though*). Have students write three sentences using either term in support of their position in Step 2. (2) You can ask students to discuss the positive and negative aspects of ecotourism as well as the effects of a decrease in tourism on fragile environments such as Antarctica.

Go to www.mynorthstarlab.com for *Notetaking* and *Academic Skills Practice*.

# ③ FOCUS ON SPEAKING

## Ⓐ VOCABULARY

### ◖ SKILLS

Review vocabulary from Listenings One and Two by grouping words with similar meaning; expand vocabulary by defining words and idiomatic expressions; use new vocabulary creatively in an oral presentation about a tourist destination.

📁 Go to www.mynorthstarlab.com for *Review*.

1. Go over the example with the class. Make sure students understand they are looking for the word or phrase that does not belong in each group.

2 Have students complete the activity individually and then compare their answers with a partner's.

3. Go over the answers as a class. Explain confusing vocabulary and elicit sample sentences from the students to test comprehension.

✪✪ **EXPAND**                                 **Suggested Time:** 15 minutes

1. Have students quickly scan the text in **Exercise 1**. Ask students if they can identify what kind of text it is (letter to the editor). Bear in mind that not all media cultures are familiar with letters to the editor. Explain that a letter to the editor is a letter from a reader expressing his or her opinion on an issue.

2. Ask students to read the text closely, paying special attention to the boldfaced words and phrases.

3. Have students complete **Exercise 2**. Go over the answers as a class and elicit sentences using the target words and phrases.

---

### VOCABULARY EXPANSION: Multisyllable Words

1. Remind students that dividing words into syllables can help them to figure out the word. Ask students to divide the following vocabulary words into syllables: *afford, controversy, depend, degrading, preserve, season, souvenir, tourist, attraction, tradition, village.*

2. Ask students to identify any common prefixes or suffixes that they see in these words. Have student pairs choose a word and/or affix to check in the dictionary to present to the class, including any generalizations they can make about the use of syllables in helping them to learn new words.

---

✪ **CREATE**                                 **Suggested Time:** 20 minutes

1. Explain to students that they will make a short presentation about a tourist destination of their choice. Elicit some possible tourist destinations and write them on the board. Point out the questions and emphasize that all four must be answered in their presentation.

2. Read the words and phrases in the box with the class. Explain that students must use some of these words in their presentations.

3. Divide the class into small groups and give students a few minutes to prepare their presentations. Move around the room and offer assistance if necessary.

4. Have students work in small groups and take turns making their presentations. Move from group to group and make notes of any recurring mistakes. Do not interrupt or overcorrect.

 **Link to *NorthStar: Reading and Writing 3***
If students are also using the companion text, you can list vocabulary items from Unit 5 on the board, and encourage students to use them in their presentations.

📁 Go to www.mynorthstarlab.com for additional *Vocabulary* practice.

## ✪✪ B GRAMMAR: Future Predictions with *If*-clauses

📁 Go to www.mynorthstarlab.com for *Grammar Chart* and *Exercise 2*.

### ◀ SKILLS

Learn about *if* in predictions; make predictions about the future using the *if*-clause.

**Suggested Time: 20 minutes**

1. Have two students read the example conversation in **Exercise 1**. Then have students find a partner and read the conversation to each other, switch roles, and read the conversation again.

2. Focus students' attention on the boldfaced parts of the sentences. Encourage students to try and deduce any rules from the examples before turning to the chart.

3. Go over the chart with the class. Be aware of common mistakes such as: If it *will keep* raining, the tourists won't come. Or if it keeps raining, the *tourists not come.*

4. Review the first item in **Exercise 2** with the class. Then have students complete the activity individually. Go over the answers as a class.

5. Read the Cape Cod portraits in **Exercise 3** with the class. Then go over the example. Have pairs make predictions using the *if*-clauses. Move around the room and offer assistance if necessary. After 5–7 minutes, ask each pair to share a couple of predictions with the rest of the class.

**Expansion/Homework**
For further practice, offer exercises from *Focus on Grammar 3*, 3rd Edition or Azar's *Fundamentals of English Grammar*, 3rd Edition. See Grammar Book References on page 198 of the student book for specific units and chapters.

📁 Go to www.mynorthstarlab.com for additional *Grammar* practice.

**◖ SKILLS**

Practice pronunciation of words spelled with *o*; make suggestions; integrate the concepts, vocabulary, grammar, pronunciation, and function from the unit to discuss and negotiate positions and reach compromises.

**◖◗ PRONUNCIATION: Words Spelled with o**

**Suggested Time: 20 minutes**

1. Read the introduction with the class. Read the words listed in the introduction and have students repeat the words after you. Play Track 53 and have individual students repeat either the entire passage or the individual underlined words.

2. Review the spelling rules in the chart. Read each word listed in the chart aloud and have students repeat after you. Then play the audio for **Exercise 1** and have students repeat chorally.

3. Have students complete **Exercise 2** with a partner. Copy the chart on the board while students are working. Once pairs complete their charts, call on individual students to come to the board and fill in the chart.

4. Have students complete **Exercise 3** individually. Alternate between having the whole class repeat the phrases in chorus and individual students say them on their own. Make the activity fast and fun.

**◖◗ FUNCTION: Making Suggestions**

**Suggested Time: 20 minutes**

1. Introduce the concept of suggestions by giving a few examples directly related to your class on that day, for example, *We should have class outside today.* Or *Let's go to the computer lab.* Also, add some weaker suggestions such as: *We could go to a café after class.* Or *How about watching a movie this afternoon?*

2. Have students read the introduction. Explain the concept of stronger and weaker suggestions. Invite two students to read the conversation in **Exercise 1**. Ask students to tell you which suggestions are stronger and weaker.

3. Have students read the examples in the chart. In pairs, ask students to take turns making suggestions using the target phrases.

4. Have students complete **Exercise 2** individually. Call on individual students and ask them to read their answers. Correct where necessary and pay attention to pronunciation.

5. Ask students to read the activity choices in **Exercise 3**. Have students work in pairs and take turns making suggestions. Allow students to make additional suggestions if they have different ideas. Move around the room and offer assistance if necessary.

## ❂❂❂ PRODUCTION: Simulation

**Suggested Time: 50 minutes**

If you wish to assign a different speaking task than the one in this section, see page 91. The alternative topics relate to the theme of the unit, but may not target the same grammar, pronunciation or function taught in the unit.

1. Read the information in the task box with the class. Tell students that the topic they will discuss is very controversial—building a hotel on a beach near a fishing village. Have students read the situation in the box.

2. Divide the class into three groups and assign each one a position to represent. For larger classes, you may need to have multiples of each group. Ask each group to read the description of their position and briefly discuss the points made. In order to prevent students from reading the other positions, you may want to photocopy the positions and hand them out and have students work with their books closed.

3. Form new groups with one student representing each position. The groups must now negotiate and arrive at a compromise proposal that satisfies everyone. Move from group to group and ensure that all students are contributing. Also, challenge the compromises if they seem not thought through.

4. Have each group present their compromise proposal. When all proposals have been heard, have the class vote for the best proposal. Students should abstain from voting for their own proposal. The proposal with the most votes is adopted.

---

## ❂ ALTERNATIVE SPEAKING TOPICS

These topics give students an alternative opportunity to explore and discuss issues related to the unit theme.

---

## ❂ RESEARCH TOPICS

**Suggested Time: 30 minutes in class**

1. Have students turn to page 194. Review the instructions for the activity with the class. Tell students that they can use a search engine (key word: *service vacation* or *volunteer vacation*) to search for information or programs that offer this type of vacation.

2. Have students prepare their reports. Emphasize that they should include answers to the questions listed in the book. Encourage students to include additional information they find. Have students present their reports to the class or in small groups.

 Go to www.mynorthstarlab.com for *Student Speaking Models, Integrated Task, Video Activity, Internet Activity,* and *Unit 5 Achievement Test.*

# The Art of Storytelling

## OVERVIEW

**Theme:** Storytelling

This unit explores the art of storytelling and techniques storytellers use. Students listen to a story told by a well-known storyteller and learn techniques for storytelling. They also create and present their own story.

**Listening One:** *Lavender* is a story told by professional storyteller Jackie Torrence.

**Listening Two:** *How to Tell a Story* is a recording of another storyteller sharing some techniques to use in storytelling.

## Critical Thinking

Interpret a photograph
Infer word meaning from context
Sequence events in a story

Analyze storytelling techniques
Complete an outline
Match actions to their consequences

## Listening

Make predictions about events in a story
Identify main events in a story
Arrange details in the story chronologically
Relate emotions to details in a story

Match storytelling techniques to purposes
Organize and synthesize information from the listenings
Identify stress patterns in speech

## Speaking

Share opinions and experiences about stories
Agree and disagree with statements
Create role plays
Practice stress patterns in speech

Use transitions to give information about events in a story
Create, practice, and tell a story

## Vocabulary

Use context clues to find meaning
Define words
Label illustrations with new vocabulary

## Grammar

Infinitives of purpose

## Pronunciation

Rhythm of prepositional phrases

---

*MyNorthStarLab*
Readiness Check, Background and Vocabulary, Listenings One and Two, Notetaking and Academic Skills Practice, Vocabulary and Grammar, Achievement Test

*NorthStar: Reading and Writing 3*
Unit 6 introduces an abridged version of the famous short story "The Metamorphosis" by Franz Kafka and its interpretation.

# ①FOCUS ON THE TOPIC

## ◀ SKILLS

Interpret a photograph; express opinions about storytelling and share personal experiences; infer meaning of new vocabulary from context.

## ✸✸✸Ⓐ PREDICT

**Suggested Time: 5 minutes**

1. Have students look at the photograph on page 93. Ask students to guess what kind of situation the photograph is depicting.

2. Discuss the title, asking the students to compare storytelling to other arts, such as music, drama, or painting.

## ✸✸Ⓑ SHARE INFORMATION

**Suggested Time: 15 minutes**

1. Have students work in pairs to discuss the questions, sharing their experiences with storytelling.

2. Bring the class back together and discuss what types of storytelling the students like best. See which type is most popular and least popular in the class. Invite students to share their childhood memories of stories with the class.

**Expansion/Homework**
In addition to asking about types of stories (books, movies, plays), you can also ask students to discuss different genres (mystery, comedy, love story), or whether they prefer fiction or non-fiction texts.

**Link to *NorthStar: Reading and Writing 3***
If students are also using the companion text, you can prepare them for Kafka's "The Metamorphosis" by asking these questions: *Do you like true stories or imaginary stories? When you were a child, did you like stories about animals? Which ones did you like? Do you enjoy horror stories? Why or why not?*

📁 Go to www.mynorthstarlab.com for *Background and Vocabulary*.

**Suggested Time: 25 minutes**

1. Have students read the caption accompanying the photograph of Jackie Torrence. You might want to give them this background information about Jackie Torrence and storytelling:

   Storytelling is one of the oldest forms of art known to humankind. Over thousands of years, people have been sharing stories to entertain audiences, teach lessons about what is right and wrong, explain questions about the natural world, and share cultural information. One of America's best known storytellers was Jackie Torrence. She spent her childhood in the southern part of the United States, where she began telling her first stories. Jackie's stories came from old American and African-American folktales. One of her most memorable stories is "Lavender," a story about two young men who meet a girl at a dance.

2. Tell students they will read and listen to a preview of a story by Jackie Torrence. Play the recording of the text in **Exercise 1** and have students listen as they read.

3. Have students complete **Exercise 2** in pairs or individually. Then review the answers with the class.

4. Draw students' attention to the picture in **Exercise 3**. Have students match the letters to the correct words. Go over the answers with the class.

📁 Go to www.mynorthstarlab.com for additional *Background and Vocabulary* practice.

# ② FOCUS ON LISTENING

## ◖ SKILLS

Make predictions about events in a story; listen for main ideas; sequence details in a story; relate emotions to details in a story; match storytelling techniques to purposes; express opinions about a story; listen to a presentation.

📁 Go to www.mynorthstarlab.com to listen to *Lavender*.

**Suggested Time: 5 minutes**

In Listening One, students hear a story told by Jackie Torrence.

1. Have students read the predictions. Then play the excerpt from the story and have students choose their predictions. Call on students to explain their predictions. Affirm each prediction as a possibility.

## ✪✪✪ LISTEN FOR MAIN IDEAS

**Suggested Time: 10 minutes**

1. Have students read the questions. Then play the story. Allow students to take notes while they listen.

2. Have students answer the questions. Play the story again if necessary to allow students to finish. Go over the answers with the class.

### LISTENING STRATEGY: Visualization and Storyboards

1. Remind students that good listeners visualize as they listen to a story. They can see the people and the story as if they were watching a movie.

2. Suggest that students divide their paper into 6–8 boxes and number them in the upper left corner. Tell them to sketch the story as they hear it to include places, time, people, and events. Their sketches need not be complex. Simple stick figures and drawings will suffice. The purpose is to help them to listen attentively and to give them enough information to retell the story to their partner.

### REACHING ALL STUDENTS: Visualization and Storyboards

- **Less Proficient:** Help students to visualize by telling a simple children's story before they listen to "Lavender."

- **More Proficient:** Have students add narration to their storyboards to retell the story.

## ✪✪✪ LISTEN FOR DETAILS

**Suggested Time: 15 minutes**

1. Ask students to read the events and see if they can place any of them in the correct order.

2. Play the story again and have students complete the exercise.

3. Draw a timeline on the board and go over the answers as a class. If there are any disagreements, replay relevant segments of the listening.

## ✪✪✪ MAKE INFERENCES

**Suggested Time: 15 minutes**

1. Play each excerpt and have students circle the adjectives that best describe the characters' emotions, and fill in the chart with key phrases reflecting these feelings.

2. Have students discuss their answers in small groups.

## ✪✪✪ EXPRESS OPINIONS

**Suggested Time: 15 minutes**

1. In the same groups, have students discuss the questions. Move around the room and offer assistance as necessary.

2. Invite students from each group to share some opinions from their discussion and if time allows, continue the discussion as a whole class.

**Link to *NorthStar: Reading and Writing 3***
If students are also using the companion text, you can bring "The Metamorphosis" into the discussion of "Lavender." Use the questions from Express Opinions to analyze "The Metamorphosis," and then ask students to explain which story they enjoyed more and why.

## CRITICAL THINKING

Give students the following questions for discussion in small groups before discussing as a whole class:

1. Who are the characters in this story?

   Answer: David, Robert, and Lavender

2. What is the setting?

   Answer: A car, a highway, a dance, an abandoned house, and a small family cemetery

3. What clues suggest that something is unusual or mysterious about the girl?

   Answer: Her name, walking on the highway in an evening dress, no last name, wanting to get out of the car at the driveway

4. Do you think the story needs more details to make it a good ghost story? Explain.

   Answers will vary, but students should be prepared to offer details or reasons for needing additional details.

## ✸✸✸ B  LISTENING TWO: How to Tell a Story

Go to www.mynorthstarlab.com to listen to *How to Tell a Story*.

**Suggested Time: 10 minutes**

In Listening Two, students learn about various techniques storytellers use and their purposes in a story.

1. Have students look at the illustration. Tell them that they will listen to a storyteller talk about different storytelling techniques. Have students read the techniques and purposes to get an idea of what the storyteller will talk about.

2. Play the audio. Have students match the storytelling techniques to their purposes. Go over the answers with the class.

**Expansion/Homework**
Many cultures have unique storytelling techniques. Invite students to share techniques they may know that are not mentioned in the listening.

◀ **SKILLS**

Organize information from the listenings; synthesize information by expressing opinions about storytelling techniques and agreeing and disagreeing with statements.

### STEP 1: Organize                    Suggested Time: 10 minutes

1. Tell students you will play the excerpts from the story again. Students' task is to listen and identify the technique Jackie Torrence uses. Point out that there can be more than one technique per excerpt.

2. Go over the answers and discuss any differences in opinions. Replay the excerpts if necessary.

### STEP 2: Synthesize                  Suggested Time: 15 minutes

1. Before you begin the task, go over the useful language with the class. Then have students work in pairs to discuss the storytelling techniques and their purposes. Move around the room and listen to the discussions, encouraging use of target language. Offer assistance where necessary.

2. Invite students to share some of the points of their discussion with the rest of the class.

📁 Go to www.mynorthstarlab.com for *Notetaking* and *Academic Skills Practice*.

# ③ FOCUS ON SPEAKING

**A** | VOCABULARY

◀ **SKILLS**

Review vocabulary from Listenings One and Two; infer meaning of words from context; define new vocabulary; use new vocabulary creatively in a role play.

### ✪ REVIEW                          Suggested Time: 10 minutes

📁 Go to www.mynorthstarlab.com for *Review*.

1. Have students complete the exercise. Move around and offer assistance if necessary.

2. Go over the answers as a class.

## ✪✪ EXPAND

1. Have students read the excerpts from the story about a boy and a bear and match the boldfaced words to the definitions.

2. Go over the answers as a class and elicit sentences using the target words and phrases.

**Expansion/Homework**

Call on individual students to read the excerpts from the story using the storytelling techniques that they have learned.

---

### VOCABULARY EXPANSION: Compound Words

1. Remind students that compound words are made up of two or more words. Because they might know the meaning of at least one of those words, separating the compounds into parts can sometimes help them to figure out the meaning.

2. Give students these three vocabulary words: *driveway, gravestone,* and *headlights.* Have them separate the words into parts and circle a word if they know its meaning. If they can't figure out the word from its parts, suggest that they look up the definition and note how each word part contributes to the meaning.

3. Have students compete in small groups to see how many compound words they can list under each letter of the alphabet.

---

## ✪ CREATE

1. Read the instructions for the role play with the class. Read the example conversation with a student.

2. Have students work in pairs to create their role plays. Allow students a few minutes to develop their role plays.

3. Invite each pair to perform their role play while classmates listen and attempt to identify the three key words chosen.

4. For more practice, you can have students repeat the activity with a new partner and new words.

📁 Go to www.mynorthstarlab.com for additional *Vocabulary* practice.

## ✪✪ B GRAMMAR: Infinitives of Purpose

📁 Go to www.mynorthstarlab.com for *Grammar Chart* and *Exercise 2.*

## ◖ SKILLS

Practice use of infinitives of purpose to summarize events in a story.

**Suggested Time: 20 minutes**

1. Have students read the paragraph in **Exercise 1**, underline all infinitive verbs, and then answer the questions. Invite students to share their answers.

2. Review the grammar chart with students and answer any additional questions.

3. Have students complete **Exercise 2**, matching actions to purposes and combining the two in one sentence. Students then take turn sharing their sentences with their partner who listens and corrects any mistakes.

4. Working with the same partners, have students answer the questions in **Exercise 3**. Encourage students to use vocabulary from the unit. If time allows, invite pairs to share their answers with the class.

### Expansion/Homework

For further practice, offer exercises from *Focus on Grammar 3*, 3rd Edition or Azar's *Fundamentals of English Grammar*, 3rd Edition. See Grammar Book References on page 199 of the student book for specific units and chapters.

### Link to *NorthStar: Reading and Writing 3*

If students are also using the companion text, you can ask them a few basic *Why?* questions about "The Metamorphosis," and have them respond using infinitives of purpose.

Go to www.mynorthstarlab.com for additional *Grammar* practice.

## C  SPEAKING

### SKILLS

Produce correct stress patterns and rhythm in prepositional phrases; use transitions to give information about events in a story; integrate the concepts, vocabulary, grammar, pronunciation, and function from the unit to outline, develop, and tell a story.

### PRONUNCIATION: Rhythm of Prepositional Phrases

**Suggested Time: 20 minutes**

1. Go over the pronunciation rules with the class. Model the examples in the chart and invite a few students to repeat after you.

2. Have students listen to the audio and complete **Exercise 1** individually. Then have students compare their answers with a partner's and take turns saying the sentences. Move around the room and correct the pronunciation as necessary.

3. Have students complete **Exercise 2** individually. Then play the audio and have students compare their answers to the recording. Have students take turns repeating the matched phrases with a partner.

**Expansion/Homework**

You can do Exercise 2 as a dictation exercise. Have students close their books and write down what they hear. Read the matched phrases. Then have students look at the phrases in the book to check their answers. Have them pronounce the matched phrases with a partner.

## ✪✪ FUNCTION: Transitions for Storytelling

**Suggested Time: 25 minutes**

1. Go over the introduction to transitions and have students read the story in **Exercise 1**, paying special attention to the boldfaced words. Then have students complete the exercise that follows and review the answers with the class.

2. Go over the transitions in the chart and answer any additional questions. Have students complete **Exercise 2**, identifying where in a story these transitions will most likely be found.

3. Have students in pairs retell the story "Lavender" based on the pictures and the vocabulary prompts in **Exercise 3**. Make sure students use transitions from the chart. Call on pairs to present their stories to the class.

## ✪✪✪ PRODUCTION: Telling a Story

**Suggested Time: 50 minutes**

If you wish to assign a different speaking task than the one in this section, see page 109. The alternative topics relate to the theme of the unit, but may not target the same grammar, pronunciation or function taught in the unit.

1. Explain to students that as a culminating activity, they will develop and tell a story of their own. Go over the information in the task box with the class. Explain to students that the story can be an original story or one they are familiar with, such as a traditional folktale from their home country.

2. Have each student fill out the story outline. Move around the room and offer assistance where necessary. Ask questions and request clarification if parts of the outline seem unclear.

3. Have students practice their story, using their completed outline. Move around the room and offer assistance where necessary. Make sure students are using storytelling techniques discussed in the unit.

4. Have each student present their story to the class.

**Expansion/Homework**

(**1**) You can assign Step 2 (practicing the story) for homework. (**2**) Encourage students to use props, costumes, and sound effects. (**3**) You may want to create award categories (for example, Most Humorous Story, Most Frightening Story, Best Actor, etc.). Students can vote for the award winners after they have seen all the performances.

# ○ ALTERNATIVE SPEAKING TOPICS

These topics give students an alternative opportunity to explore and discuss issues related to the unit theme.

# ○ RESEARCH TOPICS

**Suggested Time: 30 minutes in class**

1. Have students turn to page 194. Review the instructions for the activity with the class. Emphasize that it is not necessary for the story to be in English; the reporting task is more important.

2. Have students complete their research. Emphasize that students' research should include answers to the questions listed in the book.

3. Have students present their summaries for the class or in small groups. Encourage students to make a recording of their report that they can play for the class.

 Go to www.mynorthstarlab.com for *Student Speaking Models, Integrated Task, Video Activity, Internet Activity,* and *Unit 6 Achievement Test.*

# UNIT 7 Voluntary Simplicity

## OVERVIEW

**Theme:** The simple life

This unit explores people's decision to lead a simple life without the conveniences of the modern world. Students learn about a family of urban homesteaders who chose to live simply in the inner-city neighborhood. Students evaluate and discuss ways to simplify one's life.

**Listening One:** *Urban Homesteaders* is an interview with a family leading a simple life in an inner-city neighborhood.

**Listening Two:** *Simple Gifts* is a recording of a Shaker folk song about the beauty of a simple life.

## Critical Thinking

Interpret photographs
Infer word meaning from context
Evaluate information
Classify information

Brainstorm ideas
Apply information to new contexts
Complete an outline

## Listening

Predict content
Listen for main ideas
Identify correct details
Infer preferences based on statements

Link lines from the song to details from the
    interview
Listen for rhythm patterns in speech

## Speaking

Express opinions about alternative lifestyles
Talk about voluntary simplicity
Practice agreeing and disagreeing
Make analogies with target vocabulary

Produce correct rhythm patterns in sentences
Use descriptive language to enhance statements
Create an outline
Give an impromptu presentation

## Vocabulary

Use context clues to find meaning
Find and use synonyms
Identify variations in word meaning by context
Use idiomatic expressions

## Grammar

Nouns and quantifiers

## Pronunciation

Noticing rhythm

| | |
|---|---|
| 📁 *MyNorthStarLab*<br>Readiness Check, Background and Vocabulary, Listenings One and Two, Notetaking and Academic Skills Practice, Vocabulary and Grammar, Achievement Test | ∞ *NorthStar: Reading and Writing 3*<br>Unit 7 focuses on the Amish people and the difficulty young Amish have when they choose to leave their community. |

64

# 1 FOCUS ON THE TOPIC

### ◀ SKILLS

Interpret a photo montage; evaluate information based on personal experience; infer the meaning of vocabulary from context.

## ❖❖❖ A PREDICT

**Suggested Time: 5 minutes**

1. Read the explanation of the title and have students analyze the photo montage.

2. Have students discuss the questions and offer other examples of simple living. Ask students if they know of people who choose to live this way in their country. Note that in many developing nations, living simply isn't a choice—it's the only option. Be sensitive to this fact.

## ❖❖ B SHARE INFORMATION

**Suggested Time: 20 minutes**

1. Have students discuss the chart and the questions in small groups.

2. Call on students to share their opinions with the class. If time allows, discuss why certain lifestyle choices are different depending on the country.

## ❖❖❖ C BACKGROUND AND VOCABULARY

 Go to www.mynorthstarlab.com for *Background and Vocabulary*.

**Suggested Time: 25 minutes**

1. Ask students if they ever use online message boards. If so, elicit for what reasons. Then tell students they will read and listen to an online message board about voluntary simplicity. Tell students to pay attention to the boldfaced words as they read and to underline any additional vocabulary they are unsure about.

2. Play the recording of the text in **Exercise 1** and have students read the text as they listen. When done, work with students to explain the meaning of the words they underlined.

3. Have students complete **Exercise 2** individually. Go over the answers as a class and provide additional examples for vocabulary words that remain unclear.

⊡ Go to www.mynorthstarlab.com for additional *Background and Vocabulary* practice.

# FOCUS ON LISTENING

## ◖SKILLS

Predict the content of the listening; listen for main ideas; identify details; infer preferences from statements; express personal opinions about lifestyle choices; interpret the meaning of a song.

### ✪✪✪Ⓐ LISTENING ONE: Urban Homesteaders

⊡ Go to www.mynorthstarlab.com to listen to *Urban Homesteaders*.

**Suggested Time: 10 minutes**

Listening One is a radio report about Daniel Staub and Kristin Brennan, a couple of urban homesteaders who made a choice to live simply.

1. Play the excerpt and have students check which items they think will be mentioned in the listening. Ask students to share their predictions with the class. Affirm each prediction as a possibility.

2. Have students answer question 2 individually. Then call on students to share their ideas with the class.

### ✪✪✪ LISTEN FOR MAIN IDEAS                 **Suggested Time: 15 minutes**

1. Play the entire audio report and have students complete each sentence in the exercise with the appropriate word or phrase.

2. Call on individual students to read their sentences. Encourage classmates to correct any mistakes.

---

### LISTENING STRATEGY: Use Intonation to Comprehend

1. To show students how intonation affects listening, select a sentence and say it in a monotone. Then repeat the sentence, using different intonations to create a question and an exclamation. Then emphasize different words to show how meaning can change according to this emphasis.

2. Have students listen to the excerpt from the report, noting where and what words are emphasized. Then have them compare answers with a partner's or in small groups to see if they selected the same words and how those words helped them to understand.

---

## ✪✪✪ LISTEN FOR DETAILS

1. Explain to students that they are going to listen to the report again. This time you want them to listen for specific details and use this information to decide whether the statements are true or false.

2. Play the report again. Have students complete the exercise. Then invite individual students to read their answers. Encourage other students to call out if they disagree with the choice.

3. If necessary, play the report one more time. Give students a chance to review their answers to both exercises and go over both sets of answers quickly as a class.

### REACHING ALL STUDENTS: Listen for Details

| | |
|---|---|
| • **Less Proficient:** Demonstrate comparison sentences by writing the following sentence on the board: I use a clothes dryer, but Kristin Brennan doesn't. Then ask students to write 3 sentences comparing their lifestyle to the characters in the report. | • **More Proficient:** Ask students to create a double web, one to describe the characters' lifestyle and one to describe their own. Then have them work with a partner to write a paragraph about the differences. |

## ✪✪✪ MAKE INFERENCES

1. Explain to students that they must decide how best to complete each sentence based on their understanding of the listening. Play the excerpts from the report.

2. After students complete the exercise, invite them to share their answers with the class.

## ✪✪✪ EXPRESS OPINIONS

1. Divide the class into small groups and have students discuss the questions.

2. Call on students to share their group's opinions with the class.

### CRITICAL THINKING

Give students the following questions for discussion in small groups before discussing as a whole class:

1. What is a self-sufficient lifestyle?

   Answer: A lifestyle in which people produce most of the things they need.

2. What is your opinion of this lifestyle? Explain.

   Students can offer a variety of answers, but must support them with reasons.

*(continued on next page)*

**3.** Why do you think many families would prefer to live as the urban homesteaders do?

Answers will vary, but might include: responsibility for the environment, independence, not wanting a conventional job or lifestyle. Students should support their opinions with reasons.

**4.** What is your opinion of this couple?

Answers will vary, but students should be prepared to discuss their opinions and offer clear reasons.

### Expansion/Homework

Ask students what they feel is more important: experiences or material goods. For homework, students can research other groups that live outside the general framework of society, either in their home country or elsewhere in the world.

 **Link to *NorthStar: Reading and Writing 3***

If students are also using the companion text, you can bring the Amish into the discussion. Use the questions from Express Opinions to discuss the Amish lifestyle.

 **B  LISTENING TWO: Simple Gifts**

Go to www.mynorthstarlab.com to listen to *Simple Gifts*.

**Suggested Time: 20 minutes**

Listening Two is a traditional Shaker song about simple pleasures in life. Students listen and interpret images conveyed in the lyrics.

1. Invite a student to read the short description of the Shakers in **Exercise 1**. Explain any unfamiliar vocabulary.

2. Review the vocabulary in the box in **Exercise 2** and play the song through once. Have students identify the words from the box in the song. Then play the song again and have students listen and complete the lyrics using the words in the box. Point out that some words are used more than once.

3. Explain to students that some words in the song have more than one meaning. Play the song one more time and have students choose the correct meaning of the words in **Exercise 3**.

4. Ask students to think about imagery in the song. What pictures do the words evoke and what do these pictures symbolize? Have students complete the chart in **Exercise 4** by interpreting the meaning of the images. Invite students to share their interpretations. Encourage class discussion.

### Expansion/Homework

This would be a good opportunity to invite students to share folk songs from their own country. Students can translate the words for homework. Do the images in these songs make sense to their classmates or are the images culture bound?

## ✪✪✪ C | INTEGRATE LISTENINGS ONE AND TWO

### ◖ SKILLS

Organize information from the listenings in a chart; link lines from the song to details from the interview; synthesize information to agree and disagree about voluntary simplicity.

#### STEP 1: Organize                    Suggested Time: 15 minutes

1. Explain to students that the symbolic language of the song can be directly related to the experiences of the urban homesteaders in Listening One. Have students work in pairs to complete the chart linking the song to details from Listening One.

2. Call on pairs to share their answers with the class.

#### STEP 2: Synthesize                    Suggested Time: 15 minutes

1. Go over the example conversation and useful language with the class. Tell students they will compare and discuss answers to the questions in Step 1.

2. Ask students to choose new partners. Move around the room and monitor the conversations, encouraging students to use the target language.

 Go to www.mynorthstarlab.com for *Notetaking* and *Academic Skills Practice*.

# ③ FOCUS ON SPEAKING

## ✪ A | VOCABULARY

### ◖ SKILLS

Review vocabulary from Listenings One and Two; expand vocabulary by finding and using synonyms; create analogies and understand word relationships.

#### ✪ REVIEW                    Suggested Time: 15 minutes

1. Divide the class into small groups and give each group a letter name (A, B, C, etc.). Have each group choose five words from the box and write three clues for each word. To cut down on class time, you may choose to assign the writing of clues for homework and have students complete the exercise during the next class.

2. Reorganize the groups so that each new group consists of one student from each of the original groups. Students take turns saying clues while the rest of the students in the group try and guess the words.

## ✪✪ EXPAND

**Suggested Time: 15 minutes**

Go to www.mynorthstarlab.com for *Expand*.

1. Have students read the article in **Exercise 1**. Tell them to pay attention to the boldfaced phrases.

2. Have students complete **Exercise 2** individually or with a partner. Go over the answers as a class. Ask students if they can think of any other idioms that express the same ideas.

---

### VOCABULARY EXPANSION: Hyphenated Words

1. Tell students that some compound words in English are hyphenated, usually when they are compound adjectives that precede a noun (after-school program). Many include the word *ex-* (ex-husband) or *self-* (self-sufficient).

2. Have students work in small groups to find hyphenated words in the dictionary, magazines, or newspapers to share with other groups in the class.

---

## ✪ CREATE

**Suggested Time: 20 minutes**

Go over the definition of analogy and review the chart with the class. Then have students work in pairs to make as many analogies as possible. Invite students to share their analogies with the class.

**Expansion/Homework**
This activity can also be assigned for homework. Go over the answers in the following class.

 **Link to *NorthStar: Reading and Writing 3***
If students are also using the companion text, you may list vocabulary items from Unit 7 of the *Reading and Writing* strand and encourage students to use them in their analogies.

Go to www.mynorthstarlab.com for additional *Vocabulary* practice.

---

## ✪✪ B   GRAMMAR: Nouns and Quantifiers

Go to www.mynorthstarlab.com for *Grammar Chart* and *Exercise 2*.

### ◖ SKILLS

Learn and practice the usage of quantifiers with count and non-count nouns.

**Suggested Time: 25 minutes**

1. Have students complete the quiz in **Exercise 1**. Then have them share the results of the quiz with the class. Next, review the words in italics and see if students can guess what kind of words they are.

---

2. Go over the rules in the chart and invite individual students to read the examples. Offer additional explanations if necessary. Then have students complete **Exercise 2** and compare answers with a partner's.

3. Working with the same partner, have students complete **Exercise 3**. Tell students to use quantifiers from the chart. Move around the room and offer assistance. If time allows, have pairs present their conversations to the class.

**Expansion/Homework**

(**1**) You can assign Exercise 2 as homework. Review answers in the next class. (**2**) For further practice, offer exercises from *Focus on Grammar 3,* 3rd Edition or Azar's *Fundamentals of English Grammar,* 3rd Edition. See Grammar Book References on page 199 of the student book for specific units and chapters.

 Go to www.mynorthstarlab.com for additional *Grammar* practice.

 **SPEAKING**

◀ **SKILLS**

Recognize and produce rhythm patterns in sentences; use descriptive language to provide detail in a conversation or discussion; integrate concepts, vocabulary, grammar, pronunciation, and function from the unit to conduct an impromptu presentation.

**☻☻ PRONUNCIATION: Noticing Rhythm**

**Suggested Time: 20 minutes**

1. Go over the pronunciation rules with the class. Play the sample conversation and then invite a couple of students to model it for the class.

2. Introduce the concept of jazz chants. Explain to students that jazz chants are a great way to improve one's accent in English. They help to link sounds and to hear the sentence and word stress well. Play the chant in **Exercise 1** to see if students can find the rhythm. Play the audio a few more times. Encourage students to tap their feet or clap their hands.

3. Read the instructions for **Exercise 2** with the class. Read the lines from the chant and have students repeat after you. Then divide the class into two groups and have one group chant the long lines and the other group chant the short lines.

4. Read the instructions for **Exercise 3** with the class. Model the first item in the exercise a few times so students can recognize the rhythm pattern. Then have students in pairs complete the exercise. Move around and offer assistance if necessary. Then call on a few pairs to read their completed lines.

### Expansion/Homework

Students can make a jazz chant out of any conversation. For homework, assign a unit topic the class has already completed and ask students to come up with a jazz chant that is based on that theme and uses language from the unit.

## ✪✪ FUNCTION: Descriptive Language

**Suggested Time: 20 minutes**

1. Introduce the concept of descriptive language and go over the examples in the chart.

2. Read the instructions for **Exercise 1** with the class. Invite a few students to give examples of simple pleasures. Then have students complete the exercise and underline the descriptive language that lends detail to the passage. Call on individual students to read their underlined words.

3. Go over the instructions for **Exercise 2** and then read the example with three other students. Have students complete the exercise in small groups. Move around the room and listen to the sentences, pointing out grammar errors if you hear them.

### Expansion/Homework

For additional practice, you may want to assign a few simple sentences using students' names. As homework, students can expand these sentences using the elements of descriptive language. When they return to class, have students read their sentences to a partner. Then call on several students to share their sentences with the class.

## ✪✪✪ PRODUCTION: Impromptu Presentations

**Suggested Time: 50 minutes**

If you wish to assign a different speaking task than the one in this section, see page 130. The alternative topics relate to the theme of the unit, but may not target the same grammar, pronunciation or function taught in the unit.

1. Invite a student to read the task box. Explain the objectives of the task further if necessary.

2. Have students in groups of five brainstorm activities for each category. Move around the room and offer assistance if necessary. Be sure that students keep notes. After students have brainstormed ideas for the chart, have them write their ideas for each category on separate strips of paper and put these papers in a container.

3. Next, have each student pick a sheet of paper from the container, choose an activity and, using the outline in the Student Book as an example, prepare and practice an impromptu presentation. Move around the room and offer

assistance if necessary. Make sure students are using target vocabulary and descriptive language from the unit. Finally, have each student give his or her presentation to the group.

4. If time allows, call on students to give their presentation to the whole class.

**Expansion/Homework**

For more advanced students, write topics from all of the units the class has covered so far on small slips of paper. Students choose a slip of paper and have 5 minutes to prepare an impromptu presentation.

## ✪ ALTERNATIVE SPEAKING TOPICS

These topics give students an alternative opportunity to explore and discuss issues related to the unit theme.

## ✪ RESEARCH TOPICS

**Suggested Time: 30 minutes in class**

1. Have students turn to page 195. Review the instructions for the activity with the class.

2. Have students choose one topic from the box and research it in the library or on the Internet. Emphasize that students' research should include answers to the questions listed in the book. Encourage students to include additional information they find.

3. Have students present their research findings to the class or in small groups.

 Go to www.mynorthstarlab.com for *Student Speaking Models, Integrated Task, Video Activity, Internet Activity,* and *Unit 7 Achievement Test.*

# UNIT 8

# B fore You S y "I Do"

| OVERVIEW |
|---|

**Theme:** Marriage
This unit explores the topic of marriage and the written and unwritten agreements people make about their roles and responsibilities in a marriage. Students discuss the topic of prenuptial agreement and prepare a presentation about marriage.

**Listening One:** *A Prenuptial Agreement* is an interview with a couple who signed a prenuptial agreement detailing every aspect of their life together.

**Listening Two:** *Reactions to the Prenuptial Agreement* contains reactions from different people about the idea of a marriage agreement.

## Critical Thinking

Interpret a photograph
Interpret quotations about marriage
Infer word meaning from context
Hypothesize another's point of view

Judge the value of a prenuptial agreement
Categorize information
Develop arguments for and against an issue
Interpret a graph

## Listening

Predict opinions
Identify main ideas
Listen for details
Infer speakers' points of view

Organize and synthesize information from the listenings
Listen for contrastive stress in speech

## Speaking

Speculate about the content of the unit
Discuss quotations about marriage
Express and defend opinions about marriage
Agree and disagree with statements

Use word stress to change meaning
Use transitions
Prepare and perform an oral presentation

| Vocabulary | Grammar |
|---|---|
| Use context clues to find meaning<br>Define words | Comparatives and equatives |
| | **Pronunciation** |
| | Contrastive stress |

| 📁 **MyNorthStarLab**<br>Readiness Check, Background and Vocabulary, Listenings One and Two, Notetaking and Academic Skills Practice, Vocabulary and Grammar, Achievement Test | ⬯⬯ **NorthStar: Reading and Writing 3**<br>Unit 8 focuses on different ways of finding a spouse and diverse marriage traditions around the world. |
|---|---|

# FOCUS ON THE TOPIC

## ◖ SKILLS

Interpret a photograph; predict the content of the unit; interpret and discuss quotations; share opinions about marriage; infer meaning of new vocabulary from context.

## ✸✸✸Ⓐ PREDICT

**Suggested Time: 5 minutes**

1. Read question 1 with the class. Have students look at the photograph and describe it.

2. Read question 2 with the class. Have students discuss the title and brainstorm ideas about the content of the unit.

## ✸✸Ⓑ SHARE INFORMATION

**Suggested Time: 20 minutes**

1. Divide the class into small groups of different backgrounds, if possible. Have students read the quotations and choose the appropriate summaries. Move around the room and help students clarify the quotations if needed.

2. As a class, discuss the quotations and elicit students' opinions.

## ✸✸✸Ⓒ BACKGROUND AND VOCABULARY

Go to www.mynorthstarlab.com for *Background and Vocabulary.*

**Suggested Time: 20 minutes**

1. Have students read the definition of the word *prenuptial.* Call on students to guess what a prenuptial agreement is. If students do not know, explain that they will find out when they read the text.

2. Play the recording of the text in **Exercise 1** and have students listen as they read.

3. Have students complete **Exercise 2** individually. Go over the answers as a class and provide additional examples for vocabulary words that remain unclear.

Go to www.mynorthstarlab.com for additional *Background and Vocabulary* practice.

# ②FOCUS ON LISTENING

## ❘ SKILLS

Predict opinions; listen for main ideas; identify correct details; infer speakers' points of view based on statements in the interview; express and defend opinions about marriage; listen to opinions about a prenuptial agreement.

## ✪✪✪ Ⓐ LISTENING ONE: A Prenuptial Agreement

📁 Go to www.mynorthstarlab.com to listen to *A Prenuptial Agreement.*

**Suggested Time: 15 minutes**

Listening One is an interview with a couple who wrote a prenuptial agreement before they married. The agreement details every aspect of their life together, from who does the shopping to what kind of food they will eat.

1. Have students listen to the excerpt and then read the interview questions.

2. Have students predict the answers to the interview questions. Call on individual students to read their predictions. Affirm each prediction as a possibility.

### ✪✪✪ LISTEN FOR MAIN IDEAS                    Suggested Time: 10 minutes

1. Have students read the list of problems. Then play the listening once and have students check the problems they hear.

2. Have students compare their answers with a classmate's. Then go over the answers as a class.

| REACHING ALL STUDENTS: Listen for Main Ideas |
|---|
| • **Less Proficient:** Before listening for main ideas, ask students to listen once to identify problems. When they hear a problem, have them write it in one or two words. | • **More Proficient:** Before listening for main ideas, ask student pairs to make a list of problems they believe most married couples have. After listening, have them compare their lists to the ideas in the report. |

### ✪✪✪ LISTEN FOR DETAILS                      Suggested Time: 15 minutes

1. Before playing the interview again, have students read the statements and choose the answers they already know.

2. Play the interview and have students complete the exercise. Go over the answers with the class and replay portions of the audio if there is disagreement about the answers.

1. Teach students signal words that indicate various organizational patterns (for example, comparison/contrast, cause/effect, descriptive/spatial, and chronology). Then have students draw a four-column chart and work in groups to list signal words under each category.

2. Provide audioscripts or have students listen to several of the pieces, and raise their hands when they hear any of these signal words.

## ✪✪✪ MAKE INFERENCES                    Suggested Time: 10 minutes

1. Read the instructions with the class and have students review the quotations in Section 1B.

2. Play the excerpts from the interview, pausing after each excerpt to allow students to answer the questions and provide supporting examples. Replay the audio if needed. Then call on students to share their answers with the class.

## ✪✪✪ EXPRESS OPINIONS                    Suggested Time: 15 minutes

Divide the class into small groups, preferably of mixed nationality, and have students discuss the questions. Move around the room monitoring the discussions and asking questions where appropriate. Be sensitive to very different views of marriage between cultures and societies and be sure to keep the discussions respectful.

**CRITICAL THINKING**

Give students the following questions for discussion in small groups before discussing as a whole class:

1. What is a prenuptial agreement?

   Answer: An agreement, or contract, that the two individuals sign before they get married.

2. Why do you think Steve and Karen wanted this kind of contract?

   Answers will vary, but might include: having clear communication, having a clear understanding of expectations, avoiding future arguments, thinking about all aspects of marriage.

3. What is your opinion of Steve and Karen's contract?

   Answers will vary, but students should support their opinions with clear reasons.

4. Would you be willing to have a marriage contract similar to theirs? Explain.

   Answers will vary, but students should support their responses with clear reasons.

**Link to *NorthStar: Reading and Writing 3***

If students are also using the companion text, you can ask them to discuss these additional questions: *What do you think about having parents help couples write prenuptial agreements? What do you think about having prenuptial agreements include a rule about "group marriage" (being married to more than one person)?*

## ✪✪✪ B  LISTENING TWO: Reactions to the Prenuptial Agreement

📁 Go to www.mynorthstarlab.com to listen to *Reactions to the Prenuptial Agreement.*

**Suggested Time: 15 minutes**

In Listening Two, students listen to different speakers sharing their opinions about Steve and Karen's prenuptial agreement. The listening gives students the opportunity to recognize contrasting views.

1. Review the instructions with students and have them read the reasons before you play the listening.

2. Play the audio and have students decide whether the caller feels a prenuptial agreement is a good or bad idea. Then have students match reasons to callers. If necessary, play the audio again to allow students to finish.

3. Review the answers with the class.

**Expansion/Homework**

Ask students to think about other contracts we make in life. Is a prenuptial agreement like Steve and Karen's really a contract? Can it be enforced? You can also ask students which reason makes the most sense to them. They can also add their own reasons for considering a prenuptial agreement to be a good or bad idea.

## ✪✪✪ C  INTEGRATE LISTENINGS ONE AND TWO

### ◀ SKILLS

Organize arguments for and against prenuptial agreements in a chart; synthesize information from the listenings to debate the topic of prenuptial agreements.

**STEP 1: Organize**                          **Suggested Time: 10 minutes**

1. Have students work in pairs to brainstorm arguments for and against prenuptial agreements and find examples from both listenings to support these arguments.

2. Have students complete the chart. Move around the room and offer assistance if necessary. Encourage students to use the vocabulary from the unit.

3. If time allows, call on pairs to share their arguments and examples with the class.

1. Assign each student a new partner. Have students choose a position on prenuptial agreements (pro or con) and debate the topic with their partner using the arguments from Step 1 to support their position.

2. Move around the room and listen to the arguments. Encourage students to use the vocabulary from the unit. After five minutes have the partners switch roles and continue the debate.

**Expansion/Homework**

You can have students prepare a role play in which one partner wants to write a prenuptial agreement and the other partner does not. Have them use arguments from Step 1 in their role play. Give students time to prepare in class, or assign the preparation of the role play as homework. Call on student volunteers to perform their role plays for the class.

 **Link to *NorthStar: Reading and Writing 3***

If students are also using the companion text, you can have them debate pros and cons of marriage customs from other cultures. Be sure students are respectful of each other's customs and beliefs.

Go to www.mynorthstarlab.com for *Notetaking* and *Academic Skills Practice*.

# ③ FOCUS ON SPEAKING

## A VOCABULARY

### ◀ SKILLS

Review vocabulary from Listenings One and Two by unscrambling words; infer the meaning of new words from context; expand vocabulary by classifying words; use new vocabulary creatively in a role play.

### ✪ REVIEW                                              **Suggested Time: 20 minutes**

1. Complete the first item in **Exercise 1** with the class as an example. Tell students to ignore the numbers under the spaces, as they will be used later on. Then have them complete the exercise.

2. Focus students on the numbered squares in **Exercise 2**. Have them transcribe the letters in Exercise 1 to the appropriate spaces in Exercise 2 to complete the saying about marriage.

3. Go over the saying with the class. If there are any errors in spelling, have students refer back to Exercise 1 and make corrections.

4. As a class, analyze the saying and encourage discussion.

**Expansion/Homework**
You can turn this activity into a game by setting a time limit and awarding a small prize to the student who finishes first.

## ✪✪ EXPAND                                  Suggested Time: 15 minutes

Go to www.mynorthstarlab.com for *Expand*.

1. Ask students if they are familiar with advice columns in newspapers or on the Internet, and to explain the purpose of advice columns. Tell students they will read a letter from a woman to a newspaper advice column.

2. Have students read the letter. Tell them to pay attention to the boldfaced words and phrases.

3. With a partner, have students discuss the boldfaced words and phrases and put them in the appropriate column in the chart. Go over the answers with the class and provide example sentences to illustrate vocabulary that is still unclear.

### VOCABULARY EXPANSION: Idioms

1. Remind students that idioms are word combinations that have a different meaning than the individual words. To illustrate, give students these idioms using the word *tie*: *tied down, tie the knot, tied up, tied up in traffic,* and *tied up in knots.*

2. Have students guess the meanings for each of the idioms, and discuss them with the class until the figurative meanings are clear. Then ask student pairs to research two idioms and illustrate with the literal representation and the figurative representation. Have them include the meaning and a sentence using the idiom. Use these to begin a class Book of Idioms. Set the idioms alphabetically and encourage students to look for idioms in their daily life to contribute to the book.

## ✪ CREATE                                  Suggested Time: 30 minutes

1. Go over the instructions for the activity and the situations with the class.

2. Divide the class into small groups and have students prepare their role plays according to the instructions. Move around the room and monitor the group work, offering assistance if necessary.

3. Have each group present their role plays to the class. Remind students to listen for the key vocabulary words. When the performing group has completed their role play, ask them to reveal their target words. Ask the listeners if their words matched what the performers picked.

**Link to *NorthStar: Reading and Writing 3***
If students are also using the companion text, you can have them use the information about marriage traditions from the readings to make up a situation. Also, you can list the target vocabulary from Unit 8 of the *Reading and Writing* strand and have students use it in their role plays.

Go to www.mynorthstarlab.com for additional *Vocabulary* practice.

## B GRAMMAR: Comparatives and Equatives

Go to www.mynorthstarlab.com for *Grammar Chart* and *Exercise 2*.

### ◖ SKILLS

Understand the differences between comparatives and equatives; use comparatives and equatives correctly.

**Suggested Time: 20 minutes**

1. Invite two students to read the sample conversation in **Exercise 1**. Then call on volunteers to answer the questions. Encourage other students to correct any mistakes.

2. Go over the chart with the class. Ask individual students to read the examples. Offer additional explanation and examples if necessary.

3. Have students complete **Exercise 2** individually. Call on two students to read the completed conversation. Encourage other students to correct any mistakes.

4. Divide the class into small groups and have students discuss the topic in **Exercise 3** using the words in the box. Move around the room and monitor the discussions, giving input where appropriate to keep the discussion going.

**Expansion/Homework**
(1) To practice comparatives and equatives further, write two related words on the board, for example, *New York/London* or *train/airplane* and have students create sentences linking the words. (2) For further practice, offer exercises from *Focus on Grammar 3*, 3rd Edition or Azar's *Fundamentals of English Grammar*, 3rd Edition. See Grammar Book References on page 199 of the student book for specific units and chapters.

Go to www.mynorthstarlab.com for additional *Grammar* practice.

## ❙ SKILLS

Understand and use contrastive stress when emphasizing a difference or contradicting previous information; use transitions in oral presentations; integrate the concepts, vocabulary, grammar, pronunciation, and function from the unit to outline, practice, and give an oral presentation on a controversial topic.

### ✪✪ PRONUNCIATION: Contrastive Stress

**Suggested Time: 20 minutes**

1. Invite a student to read the explanation aloud to the class and play the example sentences.

2. Read the information in the chart with the class. Pay special attention to the three different ways words can be emphasized. Read the examples in the chart a few times to make sure students understand the difference.

3. Review the instructions for **Exercise 1**, play the audio, and have students complete the exercise individually. Play the audio again if necessary to allow students to finish. Go over the answers with the class.

4. For **Exercise 2**, read the example aloud placing the stress on the underlined portion of the statement. Then have students work in pairs to complete the exercise.

5. Working with the same partner, have students complete **Exercise 3**. Go over the answers with the class and invite individual students to read the sentences with the appropriate stress aloud.

**Expansion/Homework**
You can have volunteer pairs stand in front of the class and read their sentences from Exercise 3. Ask the class to explain the meaning of each sentence.

### ✪✪ FUNCTION: Transitions in Oral Presentations

**Suggested Time: 20 minutes**

1. Introduce the concept of transitions for both main ideas and details, and have students brainstorm any transitions they may already know.

2. Go over the answer in the first item in **Exercise 1**. Explain that the main idea presents what the presentation will be about. Have students complete the exercise individually and then compare their answers with a partner's. Go over the answers as a class.

3. Go over the list of transitions for introducing supporting points in **Exercise 2**. Be sure students understand the distinction between points with equal importance and points of varying importance.

4. Have students complete **Exercise 3** individually and then compare answers with a partner's. Allow students to use alternative transitions if they know them. Call on students to read their answers to the whole class.

**Expansion/Homework**
Bring transcripts of speeches or debates to class and have students look for transitions. This is best done in small groups. Each group can present their speech to the class.

## ✪✪✪ PRODUCTION: Oral Presentation

**Suggested Time: 50 minutes**

If you wish to assign a different speaking task than the one in this section, see page 149. The alternative topics relate to the theme of the unit, but may not target the same grammar, pronunciation or function taught in the unit.

1. Read the information in the task box with the class. Go over the topics in Step 1. Brainstorm ideas for each topic for a few minutes with the class. Then have students choose one for their presentation. Finally, have students write a topic sentence stating their opinion on the issue. Move around the room and offer assistance if necessary.

2. Have students outline their presentations. You might want to write an example outline on the board if students are having difficulties creating their own outlines.

3. Give students time to practice their presentations individually and/or with a classmate.

4. Have each student give his or her presentation to the class. Encourage students to look at the audience and use body language to reinforce their points.

**Expansion/Homework**
(1) In order to save time, students can prepare and practice their presentations at home. (2) If you have a large class, you can have students present in small groups.

 **Link to *NorthStar: Reading and Writing 3***
If students are also using the companion text, tell them that they can add information from Readings One and Two to their presentations.

# ○ ALTERNATIVE SPEAKING TOPICS

These topics give students an alternative opportunity to explore and discuss issues related to the unit theme.

# ○ RESEARCH TOPICS

**Suggested Time: 25 minutes in class**

1. Have students turn to pages 195–196. Review the instructions for the activity with the class.

2. Have students choose one topic and research it in the library or on the Internet.

3. Emphasize that students' research should include answers to the questions listed in the book. Encourage students to include additional information they find.

4. Have students present their research findings in small groups. Make sure each group consists of students who chose different marriage practices. Move around the room and encourage discussion.

 Go to www.mynorthstarlab.com for *Student Speaking Models, Integrated Task, Video Activity, Internet Activity,* and *Unit 8 Achievement Test.*

# UNIT 9

# Personal Carbon Footprint

## OVERVIEW

**Theme:** Climate change

This unit focuses on the issue of global warming from a personal perspective. Students explore reasons for global warming and discuss how individual action to reduce one's carbon footprint can have an impact on climate change. Students also analyze graphs and data related to global warming, and participate in a seminar discussing the issue.

**Listening One:** *Personal Carbon Footprint* is a radio report describing one approach to offsetting one's personal carbon footprint.

**Listening Two:** *A Call to Action* is a speech by an activist at an environmental rally.

### Critical Thinking

| | |
|---|---|
| Interpret illustrations | Classify data |
| Complete a survey on personal carbon footprints | Categorize information |
| Understand a scientific process | Read a map |
| Infer word meaning from context | Interpret a graph |

### Listening

| | |
|---|---|
| Predict content | Label a graph |
| Listen for main ideas | Organize and synthesize information from the |
| Listen for details | listenings |
| Infer speakers' opinions | |

### Speaking

| | |
|---|---|
| Speculate about the content of the unit | Agree and disagree with statements |
| Discuss results of a survey | Interrupt politely and hold the floor |
| Express and defend opinions | Participate in a seminar about climate change |

| Vocabulary | Grammar |
|---|---|
| Use context clues to find meaning | Modals of necessity |
| Define words | **Pronunciation** |
| Identify and use correct word forms | Intonation—Are you finished? |

| 📁 **MyNorthStarLab** | 🔗 **NorthStar: Reading and Writing 3** |
|---|---|
| Readiness Check, Background and Vocabulary, Listenings One and Two, Notetaking and Academic Skills Practice, Vocabulary and Grammar, Achievement Test | Unit 9 explores the topic of global warming and international and national government policy on climate change. |

# (1) FOCUS ON THE TOPIC

## ◖ SKILLS

Predict the content of the unit based on an illustration; evaluate the results of a survey; infer meaning of new vocabulary from context.

## ✵✵✵ Ⓐ PREDICT

**Suggested Time: 10 minutes**

1. Have students look at the illustration on page 151. Then call on a few students to share their interpretation of the illustration with the class. Write their ideas on the board.

2. Go over the questions with the class and have students discuss their opinions. If students cannot explain the term *personal carbon footprint,* tell them that they will find out what it means on the next page.

## ✵✵ Ⓑ SHARE INFORMATION

**Suggested Time: 20 minutes**

1. Read the definition of a carbon footprint to the class. Next, have students look at the two illustrations. Ask them why they think one illustration shows a large carbon footprint and the other one shows a small carbon footprint (big house and two cars cause more $CO_2$ to be released into the air; small house, no cars, and growing plants don't cause as much $CO_2$ to be released). Tell students that they will now take a survey to measure their own carbon footprint.

2. Have students complete the survey in **Exercise 1** and total their scores. Divide the class into small groups and have students discuss their results (**Exercise 2**).

3. Bring the class together and with a show of hands find out how many students have small, medium, and large carbon footprints.

### Expansion/Homework

Have students give the survey to students of other classes or people in the immediate neighborhood. Students can then analyze the results and draw some conclusions.

Go to www.mynorthstarlab.com for *Background and Vocabulary*.

**Suggested Time: 25 minutes**

1. Tell students they will read and listen to information about global warming—a process that is caused by greenhouse gases. Tell students to pay attention to the boldfaced words and to underline any unfamiliar vocabulary.

2. Play the recording of the text in **Exercise 1** and have students listen as they read. Go over the vocabulary students underlined. Work with students to explain the meaning of the new words and phrases.

3. Have students complete **Exercise 2** individually. Go over the answers as a class and provide additional examples for vocabulary words that remain unclear. If necessary, offer additional explanation about the word *ton*. Explain that a ton equals 2,000 pounds or about 907 kilograms. A metric ton weighs about 2,205 pounds or 1,000 kilograms.

Go to www.mynorthstarlab.com for additional *Background and Vocabulary* practice.

# 2 FOCUS ON LISTENING

## ◖SKILLS

Make predictions about the content of a listening; listen for main ideas; identify correct details; infer opinions based on an interview; express personal opinions about individual initiatives to reduce $CO_2$ emissions; complete a graph with information from the listening.

## ***A LISTENING ONE: Personal Carbon Footprint

Go to www.mynorthstarlab.com to listen to *Personal Carbon Footprint*.

**Suggested Time: 5 minutes**

Listening One is a radio report about an approach to reducing a personal carbon footprint by offsetting carbon emissions. Students learn about programs that take money from individuals and businesses and invest it in actions that reduce emissions of greenhouse gases.

1. Play the excerpt from the listening. Then have students read the questions and predict what the report will be about.

2. Discuss students' predictions with the class. Affirm each prediction as a possibility.

### ✪✪✪ LISTEN FOR MAIN IDEAS

**Suggested Time: 15 minutes**

1. Play the report and have students circle the correct answers to complete the sentences. Play the report again if necessary to allow students to finish.

2. Go over the answers with the class.

---

**LISTENING STRATEGY: Make Personal Connections**

After listening to the report, have students trace their right foot/shoe and, inside the outline, list the ways people generally add to the carbon dioxide in the atmosphere. Then have them trace their left foot and list the ways they personally add to the carbon dioxide in the atmosphere.

---

### ✪✪✪ LISTEN FOR DETAILS

**Suggested Time: 15 minutes**

1. Before playing the report again, have students read the statements and choose the answers they already know.

2. Play the report and have students complete the exercise.

3. Go over the answers with the class. If there are any disagreements, replay the relevant sections of the report to find the correct answers.

### ✪✪✪ MAKE INFERENCES

**Suggested Time: 15 minutes**

1. Invite students to read the statements in the chart to the class. Explain that they will need to decide on the answers based on what the person says. Give students a few minutes to think about the people and statements. Then play the excerpts from the report.

2. Have students complete the chart individually. Then have students compare their answers with a partner's.

3. Review the answers with the class. If there is disagreement, replay the excerpts and ask students to identify information that supports their answers.

---

**REACHING ALL STUDENTS: Make Inferences**

- **Less Proficient:** Give students a statement (for example, Private schools are better than public schools), and a list of individuals (for example, student in a private school, teacher in a public school, parent of a public school graduate). Have students work in groups to infer agreement/disagreement with the statement, based on who the people are and what their experiences are.

- **More Proficient:** Remind students that we make inferences daily based on a person's role in a given situation. Have them listen for each of the three person's roles in the report. Ask them to pay attention to what the person does (for example, Anton Finelli created the website) in relation to carbon footprints to help students with the inferences.

---

### ✪✪✪ EXPRESS OPINIONS

1. Divide the class into small groups and have students discuss their opinions using the sentence starters. Move around the room and offer assistance if necessary.

2. If time allows, bring the class back together and call on individual students to share their opinions with the class.

### Link to *NorthStar: Reading and Writing 3*

If students are also using the companion text, encourage them to use the information from Readings One and Two to augment their opinions.

---

## CRITICAL THINKING

Give students the following questions for discussion in small groups before discussing as a whole class:

1. What is a carbon footprint?

   Answer: The amount of carbon dioxide an individual puts into the air each year.

2. What does it mean to "offset" your carbon dioxide emissions?

   Answer: You send money to programs that work to remove greenhouse gases based on the amount of energy you use.

3. What are the advantages and disadvantages of these programs?

   Answers will vary, but might include creating awareness and supporting programs that reduce global warming (advantage), and being less careful about increasing global warming because you feel that you're paying for it (disadvantage).

4. Based on the discussion for question 3, do you think this is a good idea?

   Answers will vary, but students should provide specific reasons to support their opinions.

---

## ✪✪✪ B LISTENING TWO: A Call to Action

Go to www.mynorthstarlab.com to listen to *A Call to Action*.

**Suggested Time: 15 minutes**

Listening Two is an excerpt from an environmental rally to stop global warming. The listening gives students an opportunity to familiarize themselves with the language and style of a public speech.

1. Have students read the introduction to Listening Two. Explain that a rally is a large public meeting, usually held outdoors, to support or protest a political idea, or to arouse people enthusiasm about an issue. Ask students if they have

ever attended a rally. What was the rally for? What did the people talk about? Explain that they will now listen to a speech made by an environmental activist at a rally.

2. Focus students on the pie graph in **Exercise 1**. Explain that they must listen to the speech and match the sources of $CO_2$ emissions to the percentages.

3. Play the audio and have students fill in the gaps in the graph.

4. Go over the answers and replay relevant parts of the audio if there are disagreements.

5. Finally, ask students to read the points in **Exercise 2** and choose which one best reflects the speaker's core argument.

## ✪✪✪ C INTEGRATE LISTENINGS ONE AND TWO

### ◖ SKILLS

Organize information from the listenings in a chart; synthesize information from the listenings to express opinions in a fluency line.

#### STEP 1: Organize                                              Suggested Time: 10 minutes

1. Have students think about the information they would like to include, checking the audioscript on pages 210–211 if necessary.

2. Have students complete the chart with information from both listenings. If time allows, have students mingle and compare their information with their classmates'.

3. Go over the answers with the whole class.

#### STEP 2: Synthesize                                            Suggested Time: 20 minutes

1. Go over the instructions carefully with the class. Then divide the class into two groups (A and B).

2. Have the groups line up facing each other to perform a fluency line. Remind students that they should answer with information from Step 1. First, have students from Group A ask their question and students from Group B answer. Then have students switch roles. Move around the room and offer assistance if necessary.

Go to www.mynorthstarlab.com for *Notetaking* and *Academic Skills Practice*.

# 3 FOCUS ON SPEAKING

## A VOCABULARY

### SKILLS

Review vocabulary from Listenings One and Two; expand vocabulary by identifying word forms and using them correctly in sentences; use new vocabulary creatively by expressing personal opinions on global warming.

### ✪ REVIEW
**Suggested Time: 10 minutes**

📁 Go to www.mynorthstarlab.com for *Review*.

1. Have students complete the sentences using the words from the boxes.

2. Invite students to take turns reading their completed sentences. Encourage the rest of the class to listen and correct any errors.

### ✪✪ EXPAND
**Suggested Time: 20 minutes**

1. Explain to students that one word can have several forms—it can have different parts of speech. Review the first item in the chart in **Exercise 1** with the class. Point out that the word *atmosphere* is a noun and it also has an adjectival form, *atmospheric*.

2. Have students complete the chart with the missing word forms. Encourage students to use a dictionary to help them find the correct words. Then go over the answers with the class.

3. Have students complete **Exercise 2**. Call on individual students to read their answers. Encourage other students to listen and correct their classmates where appropriate.

---

**VOCABULARY EXPANSION:  ·**
**Connect with Personal Experience**

Write these words on the board: *fossil fuels, carbon dioxide, global warming, greenhouse gases,* and *carbon emissions*. Have students discuss in small groups this question: *How is your life affected by these things?* and connect the words on the board with their own experience in the discussion. Have students talk about various ways their lives are affected (good or bad) by each of these terms and then ask each student to write a short paragraph in response to the question.

---

## ✪ CREATE

1. Ask individual students to read the statements. Then review the words in the box and be sure students understand their meaning.

2. Divide the class into small groups of 3–5 students. Explain that you want them to discuss their personal opinions on issues raised by the statements listed in the book. Point out that they should use language from the word box in their arguments. Move around the room and offer assistance if necessary.

3. If time permits, call on individual students to share their opinions with the class.

### Link to *NorthStar: Reading and Writing 3*
If students are also using the companion text, you can list the target vocabulary from Unit 9 of the *Reading and Writing* strand and have students use it in their discussions.

📁 Go to www.mynorthstarlab.com for additional *Vocabulary* practice.

## ✪✪ B  GRAMMAR: Modals of Necessity

📁 Go to www.mynorthstarlab.com for *Grammar Chart* and *Exercise 2*.

### ◗ SKILLS

Use modals to express necessity.

**Suggested Time: 25 minutes**

1. Ask two students to come to the front of the class and read the conversation in **Exercise 1**. Then elicit answers for questions 1 and 2 from the class.

2. Go over the grammar chart with the class. Point out that in American English, *must* is far less frequent than *have to,* even in writing. Pay special attention to the difference between *doesn't have to* and *must not* as this is a point of frequent errors for many students.

3. Have students complete **Exercise 2**. Call on two students to read the completed conversation for the class. Have other students correct any errors.

4. Have students work in pairs to complete **Exercise 3**. Elicit answers from pairs and encourage discussion. Challenge students to give reasons for their opinions based on information from the unit.

**Expansion/Homework**
For further practice, offer exercises from *Focus on Grammar 3,* 3rd Edition or Azar's *Fundamentals of English Grammar,* 3rd Edition. See Grammar Book References on page 199 of the student book for specific units and chapters.

📁 Go to www.mynorthstarlab.com for additional *Grammar* practice.

**SPEAKING**

### ◖ SKILLS

Identify intonation patterns in sentences; practice interrupting politely and holding the floor; interpret information in a graph to prepare and participate in a seminar.

### ✪ PRONUNCIATION: Intonation—Are you finished?

**Suggested Time: 20 minutes**

1. Tell students that intonation helps us recognize whether a person has finished speaking or is going to continue. Read the introduction with the class. Then play Track 42. Ask students if they can recognize the difference in intonation. You may want to play the audio again.

2. Have students complete **Exercise 1**. Then have students compare their answers with a partner's. Go over the answers with the class.

3. Have student read the instructions for **Exercise 2**. Ask them to think of endings to the unfinished sentences and present them to the class.

4. Read the instructions for **Exercise 3** with the class. Have students work with a partner to complete the task.

5. Have students work with the same partners to complete **Exercise 4**. Move around the room and offer assistance if necessary. Encourage students to use vocabulary from the unit.

### ✪ FUNCTION: Taking Turns and Holding the Floor

**Suggested Time: 25 minutes**

1. Have students look at the illustration in **Exercise 1**. Discuss the questions with the class. Elicit that the students in the illustration are in a university seminar and that the man is trying to interrupt and the woman is trying to stop him and continue talking.

2. Go over the information in the chart. Ask students if they can think of other ways of interrupting and holding the floor. Have students add them to their charts.

3. Have students work in pairs to complete **Exercise 2**. Then invite pairs to read their completed conversations to the class.

4. Divide the class into small groups and have students discuss the question in **Exercise 3**. Explain that they should try and both interrupt and hold the floor at least once using the strategies in the boxes. Move around the room and provide guidance where necessary.

## ✪✪✪ PRODUCTION: Participating in a Seminar

**Suggested Time: 50 minutes**

If you wish to assign a different speaking task than the one in this section, see page 172. The alternative topics relate to the theme of the unit, but may not target the same grammar, pronunciation or function taught in the unit.

1. Explain to students that they will participate in a mock seminar on an environmental topic. Read the information in the task box with the class and make sure students understand the task.

2. Divide the class into groups of four or five. Have students from each group read the topics from the list in Step 1 and choose one topic to discuss. Each student should choose a different topic.

3. Explain that each student will lead the discussion of their topic. Have students read the instructions in Step 2 and prepare for the seminar. Make clear that they should not look at the information for the other topics. Move around the room and offer assistance.

4. Launch the discussions. Have each student take turns leading the discussion on their topic. Move around the room and listen in. Encourage use of target language and vocabulary.

### Link to *NorthStar: Reading and Writing 3*
If students are also using the companion text, suggest that they can use information from Readings One and Two and vocabulary from Unit 9 in their presentations.

---

## ✪ ALTERNATIVE SPEAKING TOPICS

These topics give students an alternative opportunity to explore and discuss issues related to the unit theme.

---

## ✪ RESEARCH TOPICS

**Suggested Time: 30 minutes in class**

1. Have students turn to page 196. Review the instructions for the activity with the class.

2. Have students choose one of the alternative technologies or services from the list and research it in the library or on the Internet. Tell students to find as much information as possible.

3. Have students present their research findings to the class or in small groups.

 Go to www.mynorthstarlab.com for *Student Speaking Models, Integrated Task, Video Activity, Internet Activity,* and *Unit 9 Achievement Test.*

# UNIT 10

# To Spank or Not to Spank?

## OVERVIEW

**Theme:** Punishment

This unit explores the topic of the appropriateness of spanking as a punishment for children. Students learn and discuss both sides of the issue and then debate a topic related to punishment.

**Listening One:** *The Spanking Debate* presents opinions about spanking from both sides of the issue from the perspective of parents and experts.

**Listening Two:** *Parents' Rights vs. Children's Rights* is an excerpt from a university lecture focusing on corporal punishment and human rights.

### Critical Thinking

| | |
|---|---|
| Interpret an illustration | Classify information |
| Infer word meaning from context | Conduct a survey |
| Identify arguments for and against spanking | Evaluate effectiveness of arguments |

### Listening

| | |
|---|---|
| Predict content | Take notes on a lecture |
| Determine speakers' points of view | Organize and synthesize information from the |
| Identify supporting ideas | listenings |
| Infer speakers' opinions | Identify end sounds |

### Speaking

| | |
|---|---|
| Speculate about the content of the unit | Discuss corporal punishment |
| Share personal experiences | Use language to express confidence |
| Express and defend opinions | Participate in a debate |
| Agree and disagree with statements | |

### Vocabulary / Grammar

| Vocabulary | Grammar |
|---|---|
| Use context clues to find meaning | Present perfect tense |
| Define words | **Pronunciation** |
| Use idiomatic expressions | |
| Find and use synonyms | Final s and z |

| | |
|---|---|
| 📁 *MyNorthStarLab* <br> Readiness Check, Background and Vocabulary, Listenings One and Two, Notetaking and Academic Skills Practice, Vocabulary and Grammar, Achievement Test | ⊗⊗ *NorthStar: Reading and Writing 3* <br> Unit 10 focuses on the debate over capital punishment. |

95

# ①① FOCUS ON THE TOPIC

## ◀ SKILLS

Predict the content of the unit based on an illustration and the unit title; share experiences with punishment; infer meaning of new vocabulary from context.

## ✸✸✸ Ⓐ PREDICT

**Suggested Time: 5 minutes**

Have students look at the illustration and read the unit title. Discuss the questions as a class. Try to focus on students' emotional reactions to the subject. Keep the discussion brief as the topic of corporal punishment will be discussed later in the unit.

## ✸✸ Ⓑ SHARE INFORMATION

**Suggested Time: 15 minutes**

1. Divide the class into small groups and have students discuss the questions. The topic of this unit is a very sensitive subject for many students. Some may have had traumatic experiences as children. Monitor the discussions very carefully and be aware of strong divergence on this issue among cultures. Alternatively, you can have students discuss the questions in their journals instead of in class.

2. Invite students to share their ideas with the whole class, but respect their privacy if they are reluctant to discuss personal experiences in the area.

⊚⊚⊚ **Link to *NorthStar: Reading and Writing 3***
If students are also using the companion text, you can have them discuss their ideas about the best way for a government to teach its citizens about right and wrong.

## ✸✸✸ Ⓒ BACKGROUND AND VOCABULARY

📁 Go to www.mynorthstarlab.com for *Background and Vocabulary.*

**Suggested Time: 20 minutes**

1. Tell students they will read and listen to an online parenting chat with a psychologist. Ask students if they ever participate in Internet chats and what topics they discuss.

2. Play the recording of the chat in **Exercise 1** and have students listen as they read.

3. Have students complete **Exercise 2** individually. Go over the answers as a class and provide additional examples for vocabulary words that remain unclear.

📁 Go to www.mynorthstarlab.com for additional *Background and Vocabulary* practice.

# ② FOCUS ON LISTENING

## ◖ SKILLS

Predict content of the listening; categorize main ideas; listen for details; infer opinions based on information in the listening; evaluate arguments and express personal opinions on appropriate discipline for children; listen to and take notes on a university lecture.

## ✪✪✪ Ⓐ LISTENING ONE: The Spanking Debate

📁 Go to www.mynorthstarlab.com to listen to *The Spanking Debate*

**Suggested Time: 10 minutes**

In Listening One, students listen to a radio report about the issue of corporal punishment. The report presents the case of a man who was arrested for spanking his child. Students learn both sides of the controversy from the perspective of several parents and experts.

1. Explain to students that they are going to listen to a radio report on corporal punishment.

2. Play the excerpt from the listening and have students check their predictions. Call on students to share their answers with the class. Affirm each prediction as a possibility.

## ✪✪✪ LISTEN FOR MAIN IDEAS                    Suggested Time: 10 minutes

1. Focus students on the chart. Explain that they will listen to the complete report and should focus on identifying each speaker's opinion and at least one reason for his or her opinion.

2. Play the report and have students complete the chart. Then go over the chart with the class, making sure students have identified the correct opinions. Elicit a few of the reasons students found, but do not go into detail until the next exercise.

To help students organize information as they hear it, have them draw a pro/con T-chart to list ideas from the interviews. Have them list reasons for and reasons against spanking children when they hear them mentioned in the report. Suggest that they compare their information with a partner's, and then return to a whole class discussion to review.

### ✪✪✪ LISTEN FOR DETAILS                    Suggested Time: 15 minutes

1. Tell students that they will listen to the speakers' opinions and reasons one more time. This time students must read the statements and decide if they reflect the speakers' beliefs.

2. Play the report again and have students complete the exercise.

3. Review the answers with the class. If there are disagreements, replay relevant segments from the listening and have students cite the details to support their answers.

### ✪✪✪ MAKE INFERENCES                    Suggested Time: 15 minutes

1. Read the instructions with the class. Tell students that the chart lists opinions that the people in the report might agree or disagree with. The task is to decide whether the speakers would agree, disagree, or have no opinion on the statements based on what they say in the report.

2. Play the excerpts from the report. Have students complete the chart. Go over the answers with the class and replay passages from the listening if there are disagreements. Encourage discussion.

**REACHING ALL STUDENTS: Make Inferences**

- **Less Proficient:** Have students use the general opinions on spanking from Listen for Main Ideas to help them think about inferences.

- **More Proficient:** Suggest that students listen to the report again and infer information about the individuals' personalities, reminding them to support their ideas with specific information from the report.

### ✪✪✪ EXPRESS OPINIONS                    Suggested Time: 15 minutes

Divide the class into small groups and have students discuss the questions. Be very careful to moderate this discussion closely. Remind students to treat opposing views with respect. Stress the importance of being polite while disagreeing with other people.

# CRITICAL THINKING

Give students the following questions for discussion in small groups before discussing as a whole class:

1. Should parents spank their children to teach them appropriate behavior?

   Students' opinions will vary, but should be supported by specific reasons from the text and from their own experience.

2. According to Rhonda Moore, child abuse is done out of anger when a parent loses control, and spanking is done out of love. Do you agree or disagree with her explanation?

   Answers will vary, but students should offer reasons to support their opinions.

3. Do parents have a right to spank their children without interference from anyone?

   Answers will vary, but students should offer clear reasons to support their opinions.

4. If you saw a parent spanking a child excessively, what would you do? Explain why.

   Answers will vary, but students should support their answers with information from the text or from their own experience.

## ✪✪✪ B  LISTENING TWO: Parents' Rights vs. Children's Rights

Go to www.mynorthstarlab.com to listen to *Parents' Rights vs. Children's Rights*.

**Suggested Time: 15 minutes**

Listening Two is an excerpt from a university lecture about corporal punishment. It presents the issue from the legal perspective. The listening gives students the opportunity to familiarize themselves with the style and language of a university lecture and practice academic notetaking.

1. Give students a few minutes to read through the incomplete lecture notes. Play the lecture and have students fill in the missing notes. Have students compare their notes with a partner's.

2. Go over the answers with the class. If time allows, you can write the lecture notes with gaps on the board (or use an overheard projector) and invite students to fill in the gaps with information from the listening.

**Expansion/Homework**
Allow students to use other notetaking techniques such as graphic organizers or their own special shorthand. Invite students to share their notetaking strategies with their classmates.

◀ **SKILLS**

Organize arguments for and against corporal punishment in a chart; synthesize information from the listenings to discuss the topic of corporal punishment.

### STEP 1: Organize                                   **Suggested Time: 10 minutes**

1. Have students work in pairs to brainstorm arguments for and against corporal punishment and find examples from both listenings to support these arguments.

2. Have students complete the chart. Move around the room and offer assistance if necessary. Write a list of vocabulary items learned in the unit and encourage students to use them in the exercise.

3. If time allows, call on pairs to share their arguments with the class.

### STEP 2: Synthesize                                 **Suggested Time: 20 minutes**

Have each pair debate the issue of spanking with one student taking the pro position and the other the con position. After a few minutes, have students swap roles and repeat the activity. Move around the room and listen to the discussions. Offer help with language where appropriate, but do not interrupt.

 **Link to *NorthStar: Reading and Writing 3***

If students are also using the companion text, you can bring capital punishment into the discussion of child discipline by adding this question: *If a person is abused as a child, becomes emotionally disturbed as a result, and then commits a murder when he or she is an adult, should that person be executed for his or her crime?*

 Go to www.mynorthstarlab.com for *Notetaking* and *Academic Skills Practice*.

## ③ FOCUS ON SPEAKING

**A** █ **VOCABULARY** █

◀ **SKILLS**

Review vocabulary from Listenings One and Two; expand vocabulary by learning and defining idiomatic expressions from context; use new vocabulary creatively to conduct a survey.

## ✪ REVIEW

Suggested Time: 15 minutes

Go to www.mynorthstarlab.com for *Review*.

1. Have students read the sentences and cross out the word choices that do not match the meaning of the boldfaced words and phrases. Call on individual students to read their answers to the class.

2. If time allows, ask students to define the words they crossed out.

## ✪✪ EXPAND

Suggested Time: 15 minutes

1. Tell students they will read and listen to a discussion between a child psychologist and a lawyer about making corporal punishment illegal. Play the interview in **Exercise 1** and have students read it, paying particular attention to the boldfaced phrases.

2. Read the instructions for **Exercise 2** with the class. Have students list the idioms and then match them to the appropriate definitions. Go over the answers as a class.

### VOCABULARY EXPANSION: Kinesthetic Learning

Have students work in small groups to make up simple movements that will help them remember each vocabulary word. Ask each group to perform its movements so the class can guess the word. This can also serve as a general review for all vocabulary studied by giving each group a different set of words.

## ✪ CREATE

Suggested Time: 20 minutes

1. Divide the class into two groups, Group A and Group B. Go over the instructions with the class. First, Group A students ask the questions in survey A and Group B students answer. Then have groups switch roles. Keep the activity fast paced and lively. Encourage students to move around the room.

2. If time allows, bring the class back together and ask students to share their opinions. Encourage discussion.

Go to www.mynorthstarlab.com for additional *Vocabulary* practice.

## ✪✪ B GRAMMAR: Present Perfect Tense

Go to www.mynorthstarlab.com for *Grammar Chart* and *Exercise 2*.

## ◀ SKILLS

Use the present perfect tense.

1. Have students read the paragraph in **Exercise 1** and answer the questions. Elicit any information students may already know about the present perfect tense.

2. Review the grammar chart with the class. Offer additional explanation and examples if necessary.

3. Have students complete **Exercise 2**. Then call on two students to read the completed interview to the class. Encourage other students to correct any mistakes.

4. Divide the class into small groups of 3–5 students and have them discuss the questions in **Exercise 3** using the present perfect tense. Move around the room and offer assistance if necessary. If time allows, call on individual students to share their opinions with the class.

**Expansion/Homework**

(1) You can assign Exercise 1 for homework. Check answers in the next class.
(2) For further practice, offer exercises from *Focus on Grammar 3*, 3rd Edition or Azar's *Fundamentals of English Grammar*, 3rd Edition. See Grammar Book References on page 199 of the student book for specific units and chapters.

Go to www.mynorthstarlab.com for additional *Grammar* practice.

# Ⓒ SPEAKING

## ◀ SKILLS

Identify correct pronunciation of the final *s* and *z*; identify and use language to express confidence; integrate the concepts, vocabulary, grammar, pronunciation, and function from the unit to prepare and conduct a debate about punishment.

## ✪ PRONUNCIATION: Final *s* and *z*

**Suggested Time: 25 minutes**

1. Read the explanation with the class. Then ask students to hold their fingers to their throats as described in the book. Demonstrate for them if necessary. Ask students what happens when they pronounce the sounds (vocal cords vibrate when the sound /z/ is pronounced and they do not vibrate when the sound /s/ is pronounced).

2. Go over the explanations in the chart and make sure students understand the difference between a voiced and unvoiced consonant. Elicit examples of other pairs of voiced/voiceless consonants (for example, /b/-/p/, /g/-/k/).

3. Play the audio for **Exercise 1** and have students complete the task. Go over the answers with the class.

4. Play the audio for **Exercise 2** and have students repeat the words. Then play the audio for **Exercise 3**. Have students decide which word from the list in Exercise 2 they hear. Go over the answers with the class. Finally, have students complete **Exercise 4** in pairs.

5. Introduce the concept of tongue twisters. Ask students if they have any tongue twisters from their home country they would like to share with the class. Play the tongue twisters in **Exercise 5** and have students repeat. Invite students to try saying the tongue twisters for the class.

6. Read the instructions for **Exercise 6** with the class. Have students work in pairs to complete the exercise. Move around the room and listen to the pairs, helping with pronunciation where appropriate.

## ✪✪ FUNCTION: Expressing Confidence

**Suggested Time: 20 minutes**

1. Begin this section by making a strong definite statement such as: *I'm absolutely sure Brazil will win the next World Cup.* Ask students how confident you sound. Then say: *Actually, Italy might have a chance as well.* Ask how confident this statement is. Then have students read the introduction.

2. Have students read the statements in **Exercise 1** and decide which statement is expressed with more confidence and which one is expressed with less confidence. Then go over the language for expressing confidence.

3. Ask students to read the statements in **Exercise 2** and decide whether they are expressed with more or less confidence. Then have students rewrite each sentence to have the other meaning. Call on individual students to read their new statements.

**Expansion/Homework**
You can assign Exercise 2 as homework. Check answers in the next class.

## ✪✪✪ PRODUCTION: Debate

**Suggested Time: 50 minutes**

If you wish to assign a different speaking task than the one in this section, see page 189. The alternative topics relate to the theme of the unit, but may not target the same grammar, pronunciation or function taught in the unit.

1. Tell students that, as a culminating activity, they will participate in a debate. Read the information in the task box with the class and make sure students understand the task.

2. Have students read the instructions in Step 1. Then divide the class into two groups. With a show of hands ask the class to vote on which topic they would like to debate. If you have a large class, you may need to assign multiple debate topics to different sets of groups. Have the groups decide which team will be pro and which team will be con. Remember to make clear that in a debate, they are not defending their personal opinions, but the position they have been assigned.

3. Have students read the instructions in Step 2. Have them create outlines for the debate and then practice presenting their arguments.

4. Allow each group to move to a corner of the classroom or out into the hall to prepare their arguments for the debate. Point out that they must not only support their own arguments but predict the arguments the other team will make and develop counterarguments to refute them.

5. Start the debate. Follow the flow chart in the Student Book. Time the groups. Allow no more than three minutes for each team to make opening arguments. Allow only two minutes for teams to make counterarguments.

### Expansion/Homework
(1) You may want to bring in some articles or give students time to do library or Internet research to help them find facts and statistics to support their opinions. (2) You may want to have the audience of the debate take notes on the main points and supporting information of each team, then vote on which team presented the strongest arguments.

 **Link to *NorthStar: Reading and Writing 3***
If students are also using the companion text, you may want to include the topic of capital punishment for students to debate.

# ○ ALTERNATIVE SPEAKING TOPICS

These topics give students an alternative opportunity to explore and discuss issues related to the unit theme.

# ○ RESEARCH TOPICS

**Suggested Time: 25 minutes in class**

1. Have students turn to pages 196–197. Review the instructions for the activity with the class.

2. If you can, arrange an observation at a preschool, daycare center, or other location where students can watch children and their caretakers. Students can also conduct their observations at a playground or they can watch family members.

3. Have students conduct their observations and write a report. Then have students discuss their observations with the class or in small groups.

Go to www.mynorthstarlab.com for *Student Speaking Models, Integrated Task, Video Activity, Internet Activity,* and *Unit 10 Achievement Test.*

# Student Book Answer Key

## UNIT 1

### 1C BACKGROUND AND VOCABULARY

**2, page 3**

| | | | | |
|---|---|---|---|---|
| 1. b | 3. a | 5. a | 7. b | 9. a |
| 2. b | 4. a | 6. b | 8. b | 10. a |

### LISTEN FOR MAIN IDEAS, page 4

1. b     2. a     3. c     4. c

### LISTEN FOR DETAILS, pages 4–5

Last Week: <u>informational</u> appeals
—give consumers <u>information</u> about a product
  e.g., price, <u>how it works</u>
This Week: emotional appeals
—feelings
—<u>positive</u> (happiness, love) or negative (<u>fear</u>, embarrassment)
—common, effective <u>technique</u>
—<u>feeling</u> often makes the sale not <u>information</u>
Most common appeal = <u>humor</u>
  e.g., Doggie Delight—dog <u>food</u>
  —funny voice, sound effects
  —not much <u>information</u> about the product
Effective:
  1. "Feel-good" factor = gives us <u>a positive feeling</u> about the product
  2. <u>getting our attention</u> = advertisers' #1 problem
    e.g., Neighbors' Bank
    —humor can be used with serious products

### MAKE INFERENCES, page 5

1. b     2. a

### 2B LISTENING TWO, page 6

*Answers may vary. Suggested answers:*

| Ad | Product | Emotional Appeal | Sound Effects |
|---|---|---|---|
| 1. Thief Buster | car security system | fear | scary music, window breaking, car starting and driving away, police radio, car starting and dying |
| 2. Sunny Resorts | beach vacation resort | stress | news show music, ringing phone, typing on computer, ocean, drinking, changes in voices |
| 3. White Bright | tooth whitener | embarrassment | child's and adult's voices |

### STEP 1: Organize, page 7

*Answers may vary. Suggested answers:*

| Key Ideas | Meaning | Example Ads |
|---|---|---|
| Informational appeal | gives information to consumer about the product | Thief Buster |
| Emotional appeal | appeals to feelings | all the ads |
| Positive appeal | emphasizes positive emotions | Doggie Delight Sunny Resorts (at the end) Neighbors' Bank White Bright |
| Negative appeal | emphasizes negative emotions | Thief Buster Sunny Resorts (at the beginning) |
| Humorous appeal | makes an ad funny | Doggie Delight Neighbors' Bank White Bright |
| Getting a consumer's attention | encourages the consumer to listen | all the ads |
| The "feel-good" factor | makes the consumer feel good | Doggie Delight Neighbors' Bank White Bright Sunny Resorts (at the end) |

## REVIEW, page 8

1. Humorous; factors; affordable
2. techniques; Sound effects; rely on
3. consumers; Effective; get our attention
4. emotional; emphasizes; negative

## EXPAND

### 2, page 9

1. b    2. a    3. a    4. a    5. b    6. a

## 3B GRAMMAR

### 1, page 11

Underlined words: is; sits; rings; gets; doesn't work; complains; doesn't have; is; hates; remembers; sees; has; loves

Circled words: is enjoying; is lying; sipping; isn't ringing; checking; is reading

### 2, page 12

love; is shining; are singing; are blooming; hate; wish; keeps; works

## PRONUNCIATION

### 1, page 14

1. Kathy:  Hello?

   Liz:    (Kathy) I took your (advice.)

   Kathy:  (What) advice?

   Liz:    I colored my (hair.)

   Kathy:  With Younger (You?)

   Liz:    (Yes!) It's (great!)

2. Kathy:  Did you hear about that new (flea) collar?

   Liz:    (Yes,) I'm going to the pet store (today.) How about you?

   Kathy:  I think I'll stop by (tomorrow)

## FUNCTION

### 1, page 16

a. 4    b. 3    c. 1    d. 2

# UNIT 2

## 1C BACKGROUND AND VOCABULARY

### 2, page 21

1. e    3. i    5. h    7. d    9. c
2. b    4. f    6. j    8. a    10. g

## LISTEN FOR MAIN IDEAS, page 22

1. a    2. a    3. b    4. c

## LISTEN FOR DETAILS, pages 22–23

1. department
2. diamond ring
3. home
4. file a complaint
5. forty
6. thirty
7. name and address
8. the police report
9. four
10. getting a credit card
11. don't ask

## MAKE INFERENCES, pages 23–24

### Excerpt One

2. OK?

c

### Excerpt Two

1. What are you talking about?

c

2. A victim of what?

a

### Excerpt Three

1. Excuse me?

b

2. Oh, boy.

c

## 2B LISTENING TWO, page 24

Suggestions checked: 1, 2, 4

## STEP 1: Organize, page 25

*Answers may vary. Suggested answers:*

| | Lily's Story | PSAs |
|---|---|---|
| 1. How do identity thieves steal personal information? | Thieves steal your wallet and take your ID. | Thieves get your personal information from the mail, over the phone, on the Internet, or from papers in the trash. |
| 2. What do they do with the personal information? | They make purchases in your name. | They make purchases in your name. |
| 3. What should we do if we become victims of identity theft? | File a complaint. Get a police report. Write letters to the stores. | Contact the ID theft helpline. |
| 4. How can we prevent identity theft? | Rip up receipts. Be careful with your personal information. | Get a locked mailbox. Don't give out personal information easily. Shred documents before throwing them away. |

## REVIEW, page 26

*Answers may vary. Suggested answers:*

| Positive | Negative | Neutral |
|---|---|---|
| authorize | bill | credit card |
| confirm | charges | mailbox |
| deal with | exposed | proof of |
| protect | file a complaint | identification |
| | identity theft | purchase |
| | paranoid | receipt |
| | shocking | shred |
| | steal | |
| | victim | |

## EXPAND

### 2, page 28

steal; steal everything; realize; result; find; be careful of

## 3B GRAMMAR

### 2, page 29

| | | | | | | | |
|---|---|---|---|---|---|---|---|
| 1. a | 3. b | 5. b | 7. b |
| 2. c | 4. a | 6. a | 8. c |

## PRONUNCIATION

### 1, page 31

| | | |
|---|---|---|
| 2. charge accounts | 5. Internet | 12. mailbox key |
| 3. online | 9. website | |

# UNIT 3

## 1C BACKGROUND AND VOCABULARY

### 2, page 37

| | | | | |
|---|---|---|---|---|
| 1. g | 3. k | 5. e | 7. a | 9. c | 11. i |
| 2. j | 4. d | 6. h | 8. b | 10. f |

## LISTEN FOR MAIN IDEAS, page 38

1. Jay Batchen ~~ran in~~ [filmed] the Marathon des Sables for the first time in 1999.
   OR Jay Batchen ran in the Marathon des Sables for the first time in ~~1999~~ [2000].
2. During the 1999 race, Jay ~~became engaged to~~ [met] his wife.
3. The Marathon des Sables has ~~one stage~~ [six stages].
4. Runners have to carry ~~water~~ [food and clothing] with them.
5. Runners sleep ~~outside~~ [in tents] under the stars.
6. Jay feels that the race was a ~~terrible~~ [life/special/great] experience.

## LISTEN FOR DETAILS, pages 38–39

| | | | | |
|---|---|---|---|---|
| 1. b | 3. a | 5. b | 7. b | 9. a |
| 2. c | 4. b | 6. c | 8. b | 10. b |

## MAKE INFERENCES, page 40

*Excerpt One:* a

*Excerpt Two:* b

*Excerpt Three:* c

## 2B LISTENING TWO, pages 40–41

| | | | | |
|---|---|---|---|---|
| 1. b | 2. c | 3. c | 4. c | 5. a |

## STEP 1: Organize, page 41

*Answers may vary. Suggested answers:*

|  | General Information | Specific Examples |
|---|---|---|
| **2.** How do endurance athletes feel about winning their races? | • they don't focus on winning<br>• they set personal goals | goals: just finishing or improving personal time |
| **3.** How do endurance athletes feel about their opponents in the race? | they view them as partners in a shared adventure | in Marathon des Sables, athletes share tents at night and tell stories |
| **4.** Why do athletes run in endurance races? | • to share an emotional life experience with others<br>• to achieve a personal goal | • Jay likes meeting the athletes in the race<br>• endurance runners are high achievers who get satisfaction from doing difficult races |

## REVIEW, pages 42–43

Across:
1. goal
3. experience
5. stage
7. marathon
9. finish line
10. get into
11. athletes
12. course
13. unique
14. Endurance

Down:
2. opponent
4. challenge
6. motivation
8. achieve

## EXPAND

### 2, page 44

a. 3    b. 4    c. 6    d. 1    e. 2    f. 5

## 3B GRAMMAR

### 1, page 45

What motivates an extreme athlete like Jay Batchen to push **himself** to the limit? One thing we know is that athletes like Jay tend to be risk takers. They feel excited when they put **themselves** in risky or dangerous situations. This feeling can become stronger when athletes compete against **one another**. For example, if an extreme skier sees another skier doing a difficult jump, she might challenge **herself** to do an even more dangerous jump.

### 2, pages 46–47

1. herself
2. herself
3. each other
4. themselves
5. each other
6. ourselves

### 3, page 47

*Answers may vary. Suggested answers:*

2. She pushes herself to train harder the next day.
3. She enjoys herself.
4. She blames herself.
5. She tells herself that she did her best.
6. They support each other.
7. They feel proud of themselves.
8. They are disappointed in themselves.

## PRONUNCIATION

### 2, page 49

1. Every other day,
2. The other day,
3. each other
4. something or other
5. Some other
6. one another / each other

### 3, page 49

1. d    2. e    3. a    4. b    5. c

## FUNCTION

### 2, page 50

Conversation 2 is more polite.

# UNIT 4

## 1C BACKGROUND AND VOCABULARY

### 2, page 55

1. b    3. b    5. b    7. a    9. b
2. b    4. a    6. a    8. b    10. a

## 2A LISTENING ONE, page 56

c

## LISTEN FOR MAIN IDEAS, pages 56–57

1. c    2. a    3. c

## LISTEN FOR DETAILS, page 57

1. b    3. c    5. a    7. b
2. c    4. a    6. c    8. a

## 2B LISTENING TWO, page 59

LINGUISTICS

Code-switching = changing <u>from one language or dialect to another</u>

— Speak one language <u>at work or school</u>

— Another language <u>at home or with friends</u>

Teen dialect (slang)

Parents <u>don't understand</u>

  e.g., To friend: "Gotta bounce. We gotta meet the crew."

      To dad: "We have to <u>go</u>." We're meeting our <u>friends</u>.

  Teens use teen dialect:

    — to <u>fit in</u>

    — to <u>separate</u> from adults

### STEP 1: Organize, page 60

*Answers may vary. Suggested answers:*

| Statement | Opinion | Examples |
|---|---|---|
| 2. "Some people comment on the way I speak." | Peter: A<br>Teen: A | Peter: People always ask him questions about his background because of his accent.<br>Teen: Adults often ask teens what they are saying when teens speak teen dialect. |
| 3. "Some people don't like the way I speak." | Peter: D<br>Teen: A | Peter: People often say they like his accent because it sounds "musical."<br>Teen: Parents often disapprove of teen dialect. |
| 4. "I want to change the way I speak." | Peter: D<br>Teen: D | Peter: Likes his accent.<br>Teen: Wants to use teen dialect with friends. |
| 5. "The way I speak is part of my identity." | Peter: A<br>Teen: A | Peter: Feels his accent is part of who he is.<br>Teen: Teen dialect helps teens fit in with friends (and separate from parents). |

### REVIEW, pages 61–62

2. obviously
3. intentionally
4. accents
5. slang
6. regional dialect
7. standard dialect
8. code-switches
9. aware of
10. self-conscious about
11. to fit in with friends
12. as part of his identity
13. accepts

### EXPAND

### 2, page 63

1. e    2. c    3. d    4. b    5. a    6. f

## 3B GRAMMAR

### 1, page 65

1. When I started this class, I <u>could</u> only say "hello" and "good-bye."
   I <u>couldn't</u> have a conversation.
2. I still <u>can't</u> explain everything I'm thinking, but I <u>can</u> talk to my friends and understand my classes.
3. Hopefully, I <u>can</u> take another English class next semester, so my English will keep improving.
   I <u>could</u> also try to make more English-speaking friends.

### PRONUNCIATION

### 1, page 67

1. can't    3. can't    5. can't    7. can
2. can     4. can     6. can't    8. can

### FUNCTION

### 1, page 68

picture 1: a        picture 3: c
picture 2: d        picture 4: b

# UNIT 5

## 1C BACKGROUND AND VOCABULARY

### 2, page 75

a. 3    c. 6    e. 9    g. 7    i. 2
b. 8    d. 1    f. 10   h. 4    j. 5

### LISTEN FOR MAIN IDEAS, page 76

1. F   2. T   3. T   4. F   5. T   6. T

### LISTEN FOR DETAILS, page 77

1. b   3. a   5. a   7. a
2. c   4. a   6. b   8. a

### MAKE INFERENCES, page 78

*Answers may vary. Suggested answers:*

**Excerpt Two**

Tone of voice: accepting, lucky

Word choice: "Sometime I'm tired of tourists . . . but it's good money."

Agree

**Excerpt Three**

Tone of voice: confident

Word choice: "I'm helping them to preserve [their tradition]." "They make a living from tourism."

Disagree

*Excerpt Four*

Tone of voice: argumentative
Word choice: "It's degrading."
Agree

## 2B LISTENING TWO

### 2, pages 79–80

1. a    2. a    3. a    4. b    5. c

### STEP 1: Organize, page 80

*Answers may vary. Suggested answers:*

| Effects of Tourism | | |
|---|---|---|
| | **Positive effects** | **Negative effects** |
| Pa Daung tribe | Tourists spend money.  Women are able to work less hard. | Women continue to wrap their necks. |
| Cape Cod residents | Tourists spend money. | Bad traffic.  High priced housing.  Economy depends too much on just tourism. |

### REVIEW, page 81

1. borrow from
2. agreement
3. choose
4. polite
5. enjoy life
6. destroy
7. days of the week
8. equipment
9. reduce
10. guidebook
11. change
12. city
13. open

### EXPAND

### 2, page 82

1. d    2. f    3. a    4. c    5. b    6. e

## 3B GRAMMAR

### 2, pages 83–84

2. gets; won't be able to; will probably move away; will continue
3. will probably open; opens; will / 'll be; will probably lose
4. will get; bring; probably won't be

## PRONUNCIATION

### 2, page 86

[ɑ] words as in *father*: positive, progress, economic, modern, popular, controversy, option, hospital

[ow] words as in *go*: proposal, most, vote, local, sold, ocean

[ə] words as in *cut*: month, money, company, done

### 3, pages 86–87

2. modern
3. positive
4. popular
5. local

## FUNCTION

### 2, pages 87–88

1. a    2. b    3. a    4. b    5. b

# UNIT 6

## 1C BACKGROUND AND VOCABULARY

### 2, page 95

a. 3    c. 6    e. 2    g. 7
b. 5    d. 4    f. 1

### 3, page 95

1. f    2. e    3. a    4. c    5. d    6. b

## LISTEN FOR MAIN IDEAS, page 96

1. Lavender
2. his coat
3. to Lavender's house
4. back to Lavender's house
5. she was a ghost

## LISTEN FOR DETAILS, page 96

1. c    3. g    5. d    7. e
2. a    4. f    6. b

## MAKE INFERENCES, page 97

*Answers may vary. Suggested answers:*

*Excerpt One*

a, b
"Are you cold? Would you like my coat?"

*Excerpt Two*

b, c
"It was here!" "No, it was over there."

*Excerpt Three*

a, c
"And as they lifted the coat … they both said, 'Aaah!' "

## 2B LISTENING TWO, page 98

2. d    3. b    4. e    5. a

## STEP 1: Organize, page 98

*Answers may vary. Suggested answers:*

***Excerpt One:*** c, d
***Excerpt Two:*** a, c
***Excerpt Three:*** b, c

## REVIEW, pages 99–100

1. a    3. b    5. c    7. b    9. c
2. b    4. a    6. a    8. a    10. a

## EXPAND, pages 100–101

a. 2    c. 1    e. 6    g. 5
b. 3    d. 4    f. 7

## 3B GRAMMAR

## 2, page 103

2. g    3. f    4. b    5. a    6. c    7. d

2. On the way, they stopped on the road (in order) to give Lavender a ride.
3. They asked Lavender if she was going to the social in order not to go to the dance without a date.
4. Lavender borrowed Robert's coat (in order) to get warm.
5. After the social, they dropped Lavender off at the top of the driveway in order not to make her parents angry.
6. Robert let Lavender keep his coat (in order) to have an excuse to see her again.
7. The next day, Robert and David went back to Lavender's house (in order) to find her.

## PRONUNCIATION

## 1, page 104

1. from    3. with    5. in    7. to
2. on      4. to      6. at    8. for

## 2, page 105

1. d    2. e    3. c    4. a    5. f    6. b

## FUNCTION

## 1, page 105

a. 1, 2    b. 4    c. 3

## 2, pages 106–107

**Story 1**
a. E    b. M    c. B    d. M    e. B

**Story 2**
a. M    b. E    c. B    d. E    e. M

# UNIT 7

## 1C BACKGROUND AND VOCABULARY

## 2, pages 114–115

1. b    3. a    5. a    7. a    9. b    11. c
2. a    4. b    6. b    8. b    10. b   12. b

## LISTEN FOR MAIN IDEAS, page 116

1. c    2. b    3. c    4. b    5. c

## LISTEN FOR DETAILS, page 116

1. F    3. T    5. T    7. F
2. T    4. F    6. T    8. F

## MAKE INFERENCES, page 117

*Answers may vary. Suggested answers:*

***Excerpt One:*** b
***Excerpt Two:*** b, c
***Excerpt Three:*** a, b

## 2B LISTENING TWO

## 2, pages 118–119

line 1: free      line 2: be       line 3: right
line 4: delight   line 5: gained   line 6: ashamed
line 7: delight   line 8: right

## 3, page 119

*Answers may vary. Suggested answers:*

simple: a, b
free: c
right: b, c

## 4, page 119

*Answers may vary. Suggested answers:*

|  | Meaning |
|---|---|
| Line 1–2: the gift | a wonderful thing |
| Line 4: the valley of love and delight | a situation that is joyful and good |
| Lines 7–8: to turn | to turn away from, or decide against, a lifestyle that isn't right or good; to turn towards, or choose, a good lifestyle |

## STEP 1: Organize, page 120

*Answers may vary. Suggested answers:*

1. They grow their own vegetables.
   They don't use electricity.
   They don't own a car.
   They raise chickens and bees.
   They wear used clothes and shop at secondhand stores.
2. They are free from electricity bills, cost and responsibility of owning a car, television, grocery shopping.
3. They hope that their neighbors will see their different lifestyle and make changes in their own lifestyles.
4. The urban homesteaders are happy when they can lead a simple life and spend time together as a family.

## EXPAND

### 2, page 122

enjoy: to savor every moment
relax: unwind; take it easy
change: get out of a rut; go with the flow

## 3B GRAMMAR

### 1, page 124

2. The words in italics are quantifiers.

### 2, page 125

1. a little; a few; A little
2. Many; a great deal of; many
3. some; much
4. enough; any; enough
5. How much; How many

## PRONUNCIATION

### 1, pages 126–127

**Take Your Time**

You're always in a hurry
You're always in a rush.
You always have to work.
You always have to go.
Where's the fire?
What's the rush?
Take your time.
Just relax.
You never take a break.
You're always under stress.
No time to read the paper.
No time to read a book.
Take a seat.
Close your eyes.
Take a breath.
What's the rush?
We miss your pretty face.
We want to see you more
There's more to life than work, you know.
Relax and take a break.

## FUNCTION

*Answers may vary. Suggested answers:*

### 1, page 128

a. Every afternoon; feels warm; tastes sweet and hot; feel the hot steam; smell reminds me of home; feel relaxed and comfortable
b. beautiful; shiny black wood; feel smooth and cool; surrounds me; soft and light; loud and strong

# UNIT 8

## 1B SHARE INFORMATION, page 132

1. a     2. b     3. a

## 1C BACKGROUND AND VOCABULARY

### 2, page 134

| | | | | |
|---|---|---|---|---|
| 1. i | 3. f | 5. k | 7. g | 9. h | 11. j |
| 2. a | 4. l | 6. d | 8. b | 10. c | 12. e |

## LISTEN FOR MAIN IDEAS, page 135

Problems that are checked: 1, 3, 5, 6

## LISTEN FOR DETAILS, page 135

| | | | | |
|---|---|---|---|---|
| 1. F | 3. F | 5. F | 7. F | 9. T |
| 2. T | 4. T | 6. F | 8. T | |

## MAKE INFERENCES, page 136

*Answers may vary. Suggested answers:*

**Excerpt One:** No. "Now Steve … won't be leaving HIS clothes on the floor, right Steve?"

**Excerpt Two:** No. " … we work out a compromise that's good for both of us."

**Excerpt Three:** Yes. "We can spend our time … just being with each other."

## 2B LISTENING TWO, page 137

Caller 1: bad idea, d
Caller 2: bad idea, e
Caller 3: good idea, a
Caller 4: bad idea, f
Caller 5: good idea, b

## STEP 1: Organize, pages 137–138

*Answers may vary. Suggested answers:*

| Arguments for prenuptial agreements | Examples |
|---|---|
| couples learn to talk about problems | Caller 3 says contract gets couples to talk.<br>Karen and Steve say contract shows they sat down and talked and tried to understand each other. |
| helps couples think more carefully before getting married | Caller 5 says it makes couples think before rushing into marriage. |
| makes expectations clearer | In contract, Karen lets Steve know that she expects him to put his dirty clothes in the laundry bag.<br>To avoid disagreements about money, Karen and Steve's contract states that they need to make a budget every year. |
| gives couples more time to enjoy each other | Karen and Steve say they spend less time arguing and more time enjoying each other because the expectations are clear. |

| Arguments against prenuptial agreements | Examples |
|---|---|
| makes marriage like a business agreement | Host says Karen and Steve's contract is like a business agreement. |
| not romantic | Caller 1 says that if you love someone you learn how to make them happy and you deal with problems as they occur. |
| too many details | Caller 2 says the rule about bedtime leaves no room for flexibility. |
| not legal | Caller 4 says a contract like Karen and Steve's wouldn't hold up in court. |

## REVIEW

### 1, pages 138–140

1. concern
2. occur
3. work out
4. tie the knot
5. budget
6. bothers
7. open up
8. contract
9. breadwinner
10. expectations
11. spouse
12. romantic
13. couples
14. prenuptial

### 2, page 140

All marriages are happy. Living together afterwards is difficult.

## EXPAND, pages 140–141

| Happens when someone is . . . | | |
|---|---|---|
| single | married | either |
| tie the knot<br>going out<br>proposed<br>be single | separated<br>got divorced | living together<br>cheated on<br>be in a relationship<br>breaking up with |

## 3B GRAMMAR

### 2, page 143

2. as free
3. easier
4. later
5. happier
6. more stressful
7. more difficult
8. better
9. as happy as

## PRONUNCIATION

### 1, pages 144–145

2. always; b
3. the bedroom; b
4. weekdays; a
5. three years; a
6. every week; b
7. 15 minutes; a
8. before; b
9. and; b
10. we; a

### 3, page 145

1. (Steve's) . . . twice, (Karen's) . . . once
2. (Many) . . . money, (a few) . . . other situations
3. (Steve) . . . car, (Karen) . . . housework
4. (Getting married) . . . easy, (living) . . . difficult
5. (Karen) . . . early, (Steve) . . . late
6. (Steve) . . . Japanese, (Karen) . . . Mexican
7. (One couple) . . . marriage, (other couple) . . . divorce
8. (Most) . . . verbal, (few) . . . written

## FUNCTION

### 1, page 146

2. There's a new trend in love and marriage: prenuptial agreements. You may have heard of them, but do you really know what they are? (I'm going to define) prenuptial agreements (and explain) why they're becoming popular.
3. Prenuptial agreements may seem like a good idea for Hollywood movie stars. They go through two or three marriages in a lifetime. But for regular people like you and me, these contracts are a mistake. (The) (question that I will discuss today is): "What's the problem with prenuptial agreements?"

# UNIT 9

## 1C BACKGROUND AND VOCABULARY

**2, page 154**

| | | | | | |
|---|---|---|---|---|---|
| 1. b | 3. a | 5. b | 7. b | 9. a | 11. a |
| 2. b | 4. b | 6. b | 8. a | 10. b | 12. a |

## LISTEN FOR MAIN IDEAS, page 155

1. a    2. c    3. b

## LISTEN FOR DETAILS, pages 155–156

| | | | |
|---|---|---|---|
| 1. | a. T | b. F | c. T |
| 2. | a. F | b. T | c. T |
| 3. | a. T | b. F | c. F |
| 4. | a. F | b. T | c. F |

## MAKE INFERENCES, page 156

*Answers may vary. Suggested answers:*

| | Excerpt 1 Finelli | Excerpt 2 Rosenzweig | Excerpt 3 Schoenfeld-Beeks |
|---|---|---|---|
| **Statement 1** | agree | agree | agree |
| **Statement 2** | agree | disagree | — |
| **Statement 3** | agree | agree | agree |

## 2B LISTENING TWO

**1, page 157**

a. making electricity = 35%
b. transportation = 20%
c. industry = 20%

**2, page 158**

b

## STEP 1: Organize, page 158

*Answers may vary. Suggested answers:*

| | Radio Report | Speech at a Rally |
|---|---|---|
| **Group A** What can individuals do to stop climate change? | 1. pay to offset their carbon emissions | 1. reduce their carbon footprint 2. make sure industry and government do more to stop global warming |
| **Group B** What can government and industry do to stop climate change? | 1. pay to offset their carbon emissions 2. set up industries and programs to remove carbon dioxide from the air (collect methane, plant trees) | 1. develop cleaner technology to produce electricity 2. build more public transportation 3. build more energy efficient cars and trucks 4. get factories to lower their emissions |

## REVIEW, pages 159–160

1. greenhouse gases
2. atmosphere
3. challenging
4. Individuals
5. invisible
6. pollution
7. tons
8. significant
9. offset
10. impact
11. contribute
12. emissions

## EXPAND

**1, page 160**

| Noun | Verb | Adjective |
|---|---|---|
| atmosphere | — | atmospheric |
| challenge | challenge | challenging |
| contribution | contribute | — |
| emissions | emit | — |
| energy | — | energetic |
| impact | impact | — |
| individual | — | individual |
| industry | — | industrial |
| pollution | pollute | polluted |
| product | produce | productive |

**2,** page 161

2. emissions; emit
3. challenging; challenge
4. contribute; contribution
5. Industry; industrial
6. pollute; pollution
7. individual; individuals
8. produce; products
9. impact; impacted
10. energy; energetic

## 3B GRAMMAR

**2,** pages 163–164

| | | |
|---|---|---|
| 1. must | 4. have to | 7. must |
| 2. doesn't have to | 5. don't have to | 8. have to |
| 3. must not | 6. must not | |

## PRONUNCIATION

**1,** page 165

| | | |
|---|---|---|
| 1. unfinished | 4. finished | 7. finished |
| 2. unfinished | 5. finished | 8. unfinished |
| 3. finished | 6. finished | |

# UNIT 10

## 1C BACKGROUND AND VOCABULARY

**2,** page 175

| | | | | | |
|---|---|---|---|---|---|
| 1. k | 3. f | 5. c | 7. a | 9. l | 11. b |
| 2. e | 4. h | 6. j | 8. d | 10. i | 12. g |

## LISTEN FOR MAIN IDEAS, page 176

*Answers may vary. Suggested answers:*

| | Supports | Opposes | Reasons |
|---|---|---|---|
| 1. Tyler Robinson | | ✓ | Doesn't want kids to learn because of fear. Spanking teaches kids to use violence to solve problems. |
| 2. Rhonda Moore | ✓ | | Spanking helps kids understand limits. Pain is nature's way of teaching. |
| 3. Beverly Lau | | ✓ | Spanking only provides short term solutions to bad behavior. Children learn by doing, so parents should use active problem solving instead. Spanking can turn into abuse. |
| 4. John Simmons | ✓ | | Parents have the right to decide how to discipline their kids. Government shouldn't be involved. |

## LISTEN FOR DETAILS, pages 176–177

| | | | | |
|---|---|---|---|---|
| 1. N | 3. Y | 5. N | 7. Y | 9. Y |
| 2. Y | 4. N | 6. N | 8. Y | 10. N |

## MAKE INFERENCES, page 177

*Answers may vary. Suggested answers:*

| | Excerpt 1 Robinson | Excerpt 2 Moore | Excerpt 3 Lau |
|---|---|---|---|
| 1. | agree | agree | agree |
| 2. | agree | disagree | agree |
| 3. | agree | — | agree |

## 2B LISTENING TWO, page 178

Parents' Rights versus Children's Rights
1. Rights of <u>parents.</u>
—parents have a right to <u>raise their children the way they want</u>
—under the law <u>it's illegal to hit someone else</u>
    Exception: <u>parents are disciplining their children</u>
2. Rights of <u>children.</u>
—human rights = <u>the idea that all people are equal and should be treated equally.</u>
—under this view, spanking <u>violates the rights of children.</u>
—several countries have made spanking illegal
    first country: <u>Sweden</u>
—United Nations recommends: <u>all countries pass laws to make spanking of children illegal</u>

### STEP 1: Organize, page 178

*Answers may vary. Suggested answers:*

| Arguments Supporting Spanking | Arguments Opposing Spanking |
|---|---|
| • spanking helps set clear limits<br>• pain teaches children right from wrong<br>• parents have the right to discipline their children the way they want | • spanking teaches children to fear their parents<br>• spanking teaches children that problems can be solved through violence<br>• spanking is often only a short term solution to bad behavior (kids repeat the behavior when parents are not around)<br>• children learn better from active problem solving<br>• spanking can turn into abuse<br>• spanking violates the rights of children |

### REVIEW, page 179

| | | | | |
|---|---|---|---|---|
| 2. b | 4. b | 6. a | 8. b | 10. b |
| 3. a | 5. a | 7. a | 9. b | |

## EXPAND

### 2, page 180

| | |
|---|---|
| **b.** the bottom line | **g.** black and white |
| **a.** a fine line | **h.** by and large |
| **d.** draw the line | **e.** give and take |
| **f.** pros and cons | |

## 3B GRAMMAR

### 2, page 183

| | |
|---|---|
| 2. have stopped | 7. has shown |
| 3. have . . . used | 8. have recommended |
| 4. have started | 9. has . . . passed |
| 5. has risen | 10. have arrested |
| 6. haven't taught | |

## PRONUNCIATION

### 1, page 184

1. /z/   2. /s/   3. /s/   4. /z/

### 3, page 185

| | | | | |
|---|---|---|---|---|
| abuse (verb) | lose | peace | ice | fears |
| rice | plays | niece | advise | race |

## FUNCTION

### 1, page 186

Opinion 1: more confidence
Opinion 2: less confidence

### 2, pages 186–187

| | |
|---|---|
| 1. more confidence | 6. less confidence |
| 2. less confidence | 7. more confidence |
| 3. less confidence | 8. less confidence |
| 4. more confidence | 9. less confidence |
| 5. less confidence | 10. more confidence |

*Reformulated sentences will vary.*

# Unit Word List

The **Unit Word List** is a summary of key vocabulary from the student book. The words are presented by unit, in alphabetical order.

## UNIT 1

affordable
appeal (noun)
brand name
catchy
commercial (noun)
consumer
effective
embarrassment
emotional
emphasize
factor
fear (noun)

get our attention
humorous
negative
positive
product
promote
rely on
slogan
sound effect
target audience
technique

## UNIT 2

authorize
bill
catch on
charges (noun)
clean out
confirm
credit card
deal with
department store
exposed
file a complaint
fraud
identity theft
mailbox

paranoid
proof of identification
protect
purchase
receipt
rip off
shocking
shred
steal
thief
track down
turn out
victim
watch out for

## UNIT 3

achieve
athletes
be my own worst enemy
blow my chance
challenge
course
easier said than done
endurance
experience (noun)
extreme sports
feel sorry for
finish line
format
get into

goal
have what it takes
marathon
motivation
opponent
ration
sand
set my heart on
stage
tent
terrain
throw for a loop
unique

## UNIT 4

accent
accept
aware of
bright
code-switch
code-switching
comment on
cross the line
deal with
dialect
fit in
get hung up about

identity
intentionally
lay off
make a big deal about
obviously
part of (person's)
   identity
self-conscious
slang
stereotype (verb)
stick up for

## UNIT 5

afford
attraction
commerce
controversial
controversy
culture
degrading
depend on
find a compromise
get off the beaten path
impact (noun)
in the long run

locals
make a living
preserve
season
souvenir
stretch
tourist attraction
tradition
village
way of life
wrap (verb)
zoo

## UNIT 6

approach
ask
audience
cemetery
character
chase (verb)
chilled
continue
date (noun)
dialogue
driveway
fall on
gravestone

growl (verb)
headlight
picket fence
repeat
reply
scary
social (noun)
strict
wear on
weed (noun)
whisper (verb)
yell

## UNIT 7

ashamed
consumption habits
convince
delight
fossil fuels
gain (verb)
get out of the rut
go with the flow
have a blast
homesteading
insane

local economy
natural world
produce (verb)
savor every moment
secondhand
self-sufficient
simplicity
slippery slope
take it easy
unwind
worth doing

## UNIT 8

be in a relationship
be single
bother
breadwinner
break up with
budget (noun)
cheat on
check up on
concern (verb)
contract (noun)
couple
expectation
get divorced

go out
live together
occur
open up
prenuptial
propose
quirk
romantic
separate (verb)
spouse
tie the knot
work out

## UNIT 9

atmosphere
atmospheric
challenge (noun)
challenge (verb)
challenging
contribute
contribution
emission
emit
energetic
energy
greenhouse gas
guilty

impact (noun)
individual (noun)
individual (adjective)
industrial
industry
invisible
offset (verb)
pollute
pollution
product
productive
significant
ton

## UNIT 10

abuse (noun)
advocate (verb)
arrest (verb)
black and white
by and large
consequence
discipline (verb)
draw the line
fine line
get carried away
give and take
illegal

issue
misbehavior
permissive
problem solving
pros and cons
recommend
right (noun)
set limits
short-term
take a hard line
the bottom line

# Achievement Tests
# Unit 1

Name: _____

Date: _____

## PART 1: LISTENING

**1.1** CD1 *Listen to the beginning of an advertisement. Check (✔) the best prediction of what the listening is about. There is only one right answer.*

_____ **A.** how to meet people

_____ **B.** how to remember

_____ **C.** how to organize things

_____ **D.** how to forget

**1.2** CD1 *Now listen to the entire advertisement. Use the information to choose the correct answers. Check (✔) the answers.*

**1.** People buy *Don't Forget* because they can't _____.

_____ **A.** get married easily

_____ **B.** find their keys

_____ **C.** remember most things

_____ **D.** change their lives

**2.** The tone of the commercial is **not** _____.

_____ **A.** amusing

_____ **B.** funny

_____ **C.** humorous

_____ **D.** serious

**3.** When Jim forgot his wife's name, he felt _____.

_____ **A.** tired

_____ **B.** ashamed

_____ **C.** old

_____ **D.** sad

**4.** The announcer said Jim had no fear because he was _____.

_____ **A.** using *Don't Forget* for a week

_____ **B.** forgetting his wife's name

_____ **C.** having fun at the party

_____ **D.** shaking hands with his boss

*(continued on next page)*

 5. *Don't Forget* makes people _____.

_____ **A.** feel sick

_____ **B.** find things

_____ **C.** worry

_____ **D.** remember

 6. The announcer said *Don't Forget* costs "just pennies a day" because

it is _____.

_____ **A.** inexpensive

_____ **B.** safe

_____ **C.** expensive

_____ **D.** effective

**1.3**  CD *Listen to the excerpt from the commercial about* Doggie Delight *in "Advertising on
the Air" from* NorthStar: Listening and Speaking 3, Unit 1. *Use the information
from this listening and the listening from Part 1.2 to complete the activity.*

| Advertisement | Product | Appeal |
|---|---|---|
| Doggie Delight | _____ dog food _____ | (2) _____ |
| Don't Forget | (1) _____ | (3) _____ |

## PART 2: VOCABULARY

**2.1**  *Read the paragraph. Use the words from the box to fill in the blanks. Not all the words
will be used.*

| | | | |
|---|---|---|---|
| audience | emotional | fear | promote |
| catchy | factor | get our attention | slogan |

Advertisements often include loud sound effects and bright colors because the

advertisers think it will _____ and make us remember the product.

1.

Advertisers will also include _____ appeals, such as humor, love, or

2.

even _____ to _____ their product. The most popular
          **3.**                    **4.**

products usually have an interesting or a funny _____.
                                                        **5.**

**2.2**  *Read the statements.  Check (✔) the answer that best completes each statement.*

**1.** To be *affordable* means to be _____.

_____ **A.** cheap                    _____ **C.** popular

_____ **B.** expensive                _____ **D.** successful

**2.** An *embarrassment* is a/an _____.

_____ **A.** informational appeal     _____ **C.** proud feeling

_____ **B.** positive emotion         _____ **D.** uncomfortable moment

**3.** A *consumer* is a person who _____.

_____ **A.** creates advertisements   _____ **C.** purchases products

_____ **B.** makes commercials        _____ **D.** sells information

**4.** To *rely on* a product means to _____ the product.

_____ **A.** build on                 _____ **C.** depend on

_____ **B.** buy                      _____ **D.** ignore

**5.** To be *effective* means to be _____.

_____ **A.** appealing                _____ **C.** easy

_____ **B.** creative                 _____ **D.** useful

## PART 3: SKILLS FOR SPEAKING

**3.1**  *Complete the commercial.  Fill in the blanks using the simple present or present progressive.*

Do you _____ trouble remembering things? Now there is a
            **1. (have)**

solution—this little pill called *Don't Forget*. It is so effective you'll never suffer the

embarrassment that Jim did. Look at Jim now, after using *Don't Forget* for one

week. He is at a party, and he _____ hands with his boss. With no
                                        **2. (shake)**

fear, he _____ his wife, Elena. It _____ like Jim will
              **3. (introduce)**                    **4. (look)**

finally be happy now!

**T-3**

**3.2**  CD 7  *Listen to the conversation. Circle the part of the conversation where the speaker highlights important information.*

ELENA: Do you remember what (today) is, Jim?
JIM:       It's Wednesday. Why?
ELENA: Yeah, and it's also our anniversary.
JIM:       Really? I need more *Don't Forget.*

**3.3**  *Read the attention grabbers. Check (✔) the technique used for each statement.*

1. "Do you have trouble remembering things? You can't remember where you put your keys, your watch, or even the glasses on top of your head?"

   _____ **A.** Ask a question.

   _____ **B.** Give a solution to a problem.

   _____ **C.** Give a dramatic fact or statistic.

   _____ **D.** Tell an anecdote.

2. "I just can't emphasize enough how this pill has changed my life. I have four kids and before I took this pill, I couldn't even remember their names!"

   _____ **A.** Ask a question.

   _____ **B.** Give a solution to a problem.

   _____ **C.** Give a dramatic fact or statistic.

   _____ **D.** Tell an anecdote.

3. "Over 1 million people in the United States have tried *Don't Forget* and all of them say it's the best choice they've ever made."

   _____ **A.** Ask a question.

   _____ **B.** Give a solution to a problem.

   _____ **C.** Give a dramatic fact or statistic.

   _____ **D.** Tell an anecdote.

## PART 4: SPEAKING

**4.1**  *The commercial in Part 1.2 uses one type of appeal. What type is it? Check (✔) the best answer. You may listen again to Part 1.2.*

The *Don't Forget* commercial uses the following appeal:

_____ **A.** Positive        _____ **B.** Negative        _____ **C.** Neither

**4.2** *Say a new attention grabber that could be used to replace the old one for* Don't Forget—It's the one thing you'll always remember.

**4.3** *Making an Advertisement*

*Speak for 1–2 minutes. Imagine a new commercial for* Don't Forget. *Describe your commercial.*

- Take notes.
- Refer to the product name and the new attention grabber.
- Use the simple present tense and the present progressive.
- Emphasize certain words to make your meaning clear.
- Use attention grabbers to get your listeners' attention.
- Use the vocabulary and grammar from Unit 1.

| Unit 1 Vocabulary Words | | | |
|---|---|---|---|
| affordable | effective | fear | promote |
| catchy | embarrassment | humorous | rely on |
| consumers | factors | negative | |

| Unit 1 Grammar: Simple Present and Present Progressive |
|---|
| [simple present]<br>• He **buys** that dog food every day.<br><br>[present progressive]<br>• He **is buying** the food at the store right now. |

# Achievement Tests
# Unit 2

Name: _____

Date: _____

## PART 1: LISTENING

**1.1** *Listen to the beginning of a phone recording. Check (✔) the best prediction of what the listening is about. There is only one right answer.*

_____ **A.** the IdentiTrue company

_____ **B.** a victim of identity theft

_____ **C.** how to contact the police

_____ **D.** how to plan identity theft

**1.2** *Now listen to the entire phone recording. Use the information to choose the correct answers. Check (✔) the answers.*

1. How does the IdentiTrue information line help victims of identity theft?

   _____ **A.** It promises to track down any thieves who steal.

   _____ **B.** It contacts the local police department about the theft.

   _____ **C.** It helps people understand and prevent identity theft.

   _____ **D.** It gives people money if their wallet has been stolen.

2. Greta called IdentiTrue because her _____ was stolen.

   _____ **A.** car

   _____ **B.** credit card

   _____ **C.** money

   _____ **D.** purse

3. Greta asked, "Who would take a library card?!" because she felt

   _____.

   _____ **A.** excited

   _____ **B.** exposed

   _____ **C.** paranoid

   _____ **D.** shocked

4. The thief bought _____ worth of baby clothes.

   _____ **A.** $5

   _____ **B.** $15

   _____ **C.** $50

   _____ **D.** $500

5. The police told Greta to call the IdentiTrue information line to

_____.

_____ **A.** learn more about protecting herself

_____ **B.** see if her credit cards were found

_____ **C.** report her missing cell phone

_____ **D.** file a complaint about the theft

6. Based on the listening, which would Greta *agree* with?

_____ **A.** the department store helped her

_____ **B.** the police department helped her

_____ **C.** the local library helped her

_____ **D.** the information line helped her

**1.3** ⊂ᴰ⁷ *Listen to the excerpt from "Lily's Story" from* NorthStar: Listening and Speaking 3,
   ⑧ *Unit 2. Compare the information from this listening and the listening from Part 1.2
   to complete the activity. Not all items will be used.*

~~A. called the IdentiTrue information line for help~~

**B.** was charged for something that she didn't buy

**C.** was not concerned about the identity theft

**D.** found the person who had stolen her identity

**E.** had no idea that she was an identity theft victim

**F.** found out that someone broke into her car

| Identity Theft Stories | | |
|---|---|---|
| **Lily** | **Greta** | **Both** |
| I. | A<br><br>2. | 3. |

## PART 2: VOCABULARY

**2.1**  *Decide if each word has a meaning that is positive (good), negative (bad), or neutral (neither good nor bad). Write* Positive, Negative, *or* Neither *next to each word.*

_____ **1.** authorize

_____ **2.** safe

_____ **3.** department store

_____ **4.** paranoid

_____ **5.** receipt

_____ **6.** rip off

**2.2**  *Read the e-mail from Carl to his friend Mark. Check (✔) the word that is <u>not</u> similar to the word from the e-mail. There is only one right answer.*

To: markymark@gmail.com
From: coolcarl2@hotmail.com
Subject: Money

Hey Mark!

Remember when I used my credit card to buy things on the Internet last week? Well, I looked at my bank account and found <u>charges</u> for 10 baseball tickets and a new guitar. I didn't buy those things! So, I called the police to <u>file a complaint</u>. They told me that 1 out of every 5 people is a <u>victim</u> of <u>identity theft</u>. I feel so <u>exposed</u> by this whole situation.

Anyway, I wanted to ask if I could borrow some money from you. I'll pay you back after I <u>deal with</u> this first. Is that okay?

Carl

|   | identity theft | ____ stealing | ✔ account | ____ crime |
|---|---|---|---|---|
| **1.** | charges | ____ bills | ____ payments | ____ products |
| **2.** | file a complaint | ____ accept | ____ argue | ____ complain |
| **3.** | victim | ____ sufferer | ____ criminal | ____ target |
| **4.** | exposed | ____ protected | ____ revealed | ____ unsafe |
| **5.** | deal with | ____ avoid | ____ control | ____ manage |

## PART 3: SKILLS FOR SPEAKING

**3.1**   *Complete the conversations with the correct modals of advice. Check (✔) the answers.*

CARL:   I got a bill for charges that I didn't even make.
GRETA:   _____.

✔ A.  Well, you ought to file a complaint.

_____ B.  Well, you should to file a complaint.

_____ C.  Well, you had better to file a complaint.

1.  GRETA:  I always leave my wallet in my desk at the office.
CARL:   _____.

_____ A.  You ought better buy a lock for the desk.

_____ B.  You had better buy a lock for the desk.

_____ C.  You should better buy a lock for the desk.

2.  GRETA:  Mark's boss asked about his password for his e-mail account.
CARL:   _____.

_____ A.  He hadn't better not give the password.

_____ B.  He shouldn't not give the password.

_____ C.  He had better not give the password.

3.  CARL:   Mark told me you just got your passport.
GRETA:   _____.

_____ A.  Yeah, I ought to lose it.

_____ B.  Yeah, I had better lose it.

_____ C.  Yeah, I shouldn't lose it.

**3.2**   ᶜ ᴰ ⁷  *Listen to the compound nouns. Circle the part of the compound noun with the heaviest stress and highest pitch.*

five thousand (dollars)

1.  credit cards

2.  identity theft victim

3.  checkbook

**3.3**  ᶜ ᴰ ₇ *Listen to the conversation between Lily and Carl.  Circle the parts of the*
    🔟  *conversation where Carl keeps the conversation going.*

LILY:   Yesterday, I went to the grocery store and some guy tried to steal my purse.
CARL:   And?
LILY:   Well, some woman came over to help me and the guy just ran away.
CARL:   So, what happened next?
LILY:   He just kept running and the woman called the police for me.
CARL:   Wow! I can't believe he did that.
LILY:   Yeah. I need to be more careful, I guess.
CARL:   I guess so.

## PART 4:  SPEAKING

**4.1**  *Is the statement below true, false, or not given?  Check (✔) the answer. You may listen*
    *again to Part 1.2.*

Greta's phone message is about her experience with identity theft.

_____ **A.** True          _____ **B.** False          _____ **C.** Not given

**4.2**  *Write two kinds of advice that you would give to Greta. Then tell your advice to a*
    *partner.  Use these expressions:*

                    She should . . .
                    She ought to . . .
                    She had better . . .
                    She shouldn't . . .

**4.3**   *Giving Advice*

*Speak for 1–2 minutes. Explain what you would tell a friend to do if he/she were a victim of identity theft.*

- Take notes.
- Give 2 kinds of advice suggesting what your friend should do.
- Use modals of advice.
- Use the vocabulary and grammar from Unit 2.

| Unit 2 Vocabulary Words | | | |
|---|---|---|---|
| authorize | department store | paranoid | rip off |
| charges | exposed | purchase | victim |
| confirm | file a complaint | receipt | watch out for |
| deal with | | | |

| Unit 2 Grammar:  Modals of Advice |
|---|
| • You ***should*** call the police right away. |

## PART 1: LISTENING

**1.1** CD 1 / 11 *Listen to the beginning of a speech. Check (✔) the best prediction of what the speech is about. There is only one right answer.*

_____ **A.** the man's two children

_____ **B.** terrible diseases

_____ **C.** the loss of his loved ones

_____ **D.** the man's exercise experience

**1.2** CD 1 / 12 *Now listen to the entire speech. Use the information to choose the correct answers. Check (✔) the answers.*

**1.** The man's speech was about _____.

_____ **A.** his new book on running races

_____ **B.** setting goals and reaching them

_____ **C.** the challenges of having children

_____ **D.** the difficulties in everyday life

**2.** He walked for _____ minutes the first day he started exercising.

_____ **A.** 10

_____ **B.** 15

_____ **C.** 20

_____ **D.** 30

**3.** What did he mean when he said "I think having [people] with me through those 26 miles helped me finish"?

_____ **A.** They cheered for him on TV.

_____ **B.** They gave him food and water.

_____ **C.** They ran the race with him.

_____ **D.** They supported his running goals.

**4.** The man said that he finished a _____ mile race.

_____ **A.** sixteen

_____ **B.** twenty

_____ **C.** twenty-six

_____ **D.** thirty-six

   **5.** How many pounds did he lose in his first year of running?

       _____ **A.** 50

       _____ **B.** 100

       _____ **C.** 150

       _____ **D.** 200

   **6.** The man thinks that people need _____ to be successful.

       _____ **A.** a good attitude

       _____ **B.** a strong heart

       _____ **C.** to run a race

       _____ **D.** to start walking

**1.3**  CD1 13  *Listen to the excerpt from "Ultrarunner Jay Batchen" from* NorthStar: Listening and Speaking 3, *Unit 3. Use the information from this listening and the listening from Part 1.2 to complete the activity. Not all items will be used in chart.*

   **A.** ~~Runs long, difficult races~~

   **B.** Enters contests to make money

   **C.** Runs to be healthy

   **D.** Runs to meet new people

   **E.** Wants to be famous

   **F.** Wants to help others do well

| Jay Batchen | Runner in Part 1 | Both |
|---|---|---|
| 1. | 2. | A |
| | 3. | |

## PART 2: VOCABULARY

**2.1**  *Read the sentences. Use the words from the box to fill in the blanks. Not all the words will be used.*

| | | | |
|---|---|---|---|
| achieve | course | finish line | set my heart on |
| challenge | endurance | motivation | terrain |

1. This was not the _____ that I wanted my life to take, but what could I do?

2. Some days I was so sad and tired that it was a _____ just to get off the couch.

3. Soon my _____ improved, and I felt so good—mentally and physically—that I even began running.

4. After one year of running, I was able to _____ my dream: I completed a marathon!

5. For each mile of hot mountain _____, I kept myself going by thinking of a different person.

**2.2**  *Read the statements. Check (✔) the answer that best completes each statement.*

1. To *throw someone for a loop* means to _____.

    _____ **A.** confuse

    _____ **B.** scare

    _____ **C.** hurt

    _____ **D.** worry

2. To *blow your chance* means to _____.

    _____ **A.** do something differently

    _____ **B.** have a bad experience

    _____ **C.** lose the opportunity

    _____ **D.** try something again

3. To *get into* a sport means to _____ that sport.

   _____ **A.** begin

   _____ **B.** finish

   _____ **C.** ignore

   _____ **D.** support

4. A *marathon* is a _____.

   _____ **A.** short race

   _____ **B.** long race

   _____ **C.** special prize

   _____ **D.** type of athlete

5. To *feel sorry for* a person means to feel _____ for him or her.

   _____ **A.** bad

   _____ **B.** happy

   _____ **C.** puzzled

   _____ **D.** scared

## PART 3: SKILLS FOR SPEAKING

**3.1**  *Complete the paragraph. Fill in the blanks using reflexive pronouns.*

When I am running, sometimes I have to remind __myself__ that I am doing this to

stay healthy. My wife doesn't seem to understand this, but she has never tried

running _____. So, I don't think she would know what I mean. You just have to
            **1.**

ask _____, "Is this good for my body?" I tell _____ that it is because I look
      **2.**                                            **3.**

and feel great! We should all think about getting _____ into shape too.
                                                      **4.**

**3.2**  CD7 (14) *Listen to the sentences. Use the expressions with* other *from the box to fill in the blanks.*

| | | | |
|---|---|---|---|
| another | each other | ~~something or other~~ | the other night |

He ate __*something or other*__ and felt sick.

1. We went to a great party _____.

2. They argue with _____ all the time.

3. I want to live alone. I don't want _____ roommate.

**3.3**  *Read the sentences. Write* S *for a strong opinion,* W *for a weak opinion, and* N *if it is not an opinion sentence.*

___N___  A marathon is a 26-mile race.

_____ **1.** I think having them with me through the race helped me to finish.

_____ **2.** It seems like people would be happier and healthier if they ran more.

_____ **3.** I'm pretty sure my story can inspire others to keep a positive attitude.

## PART 4: SPEAKING

**4.1**  *Say an aphorism that you would use to describe your attitude. Example:*

My favorite saying is *"You can soar on the wings of an optimistic attitude."*

**4.2**  *Say one brief opinion statement about why you chose that aphorism.*

I think that . . . / I believe that . . .
_____

**4.3** *Sharing Your Hobby*

*Speak for 1–2 minutes. Explain an activity (e.g., playing sports, dancing, playing music) that you enjoy doing.*

- Take notes.
- Refer to the listening from Part 1.2.
- Include your personal aphorism and your opinion.
- Use reflexive and reciprocal pronouns.
- Use expressions with *other*.
- Use the vocabulary and grammar from Unit 3.

<table>
<tr><td colspan="4" align="center">Unit 3 Vocabulary Words</td></tr>
<tr>
<td>achieve<br>blow my chance<br>challenge</td>
<td>easier said than done<br>endurance<br>experience</td>
<td>feel sorry for<br>get into<br>opponent</td>
<td>set my heart on<br>unique</td>
</tr>
<tr><td colspan="4" align="center">Unit 3 Grammar: Reflexive Pronouns</td></tr>
<tr><td colspan="4" align="center">• I would never join a team by myself.</td></tr>
</table>

# Achievement Tests
# Unit 4

Name: _____

Date: _____

## PART 1: LISTENING

**1.1** 🔊 *Listen to the beginning of a classroom discussion. Check (✔) the meaning of*
15 *accent. There is only one right answer.*

_____ **A.** the way people act when talking with others

_____ **B.** the way people fit in when talking with others

_____ **C.** the way people look when talking with others

_____ **D.** the way people sound when talking with others

**1.2** 🔊 *Now listen to the entire discussion. Use the information to choose the correct*
16 *answers. Check (✔) the answers.*

1. The discussion is about how accents affect people's _____.

_____ **A.** dialects

_____ **B.** identities

_____ **C.** parents

_____ **D.** slang

2. The professor says that many children want to _____ their
parents.

_____ **A.** dress the same as

_____ **B.** fit in with

_____ **C.** separate from

_____ **D.** speak like

3. Maria thinks that a lot of _____ use slang words.

_____ **A.** babies

_____ **B.** children

_____ **C.** parents

_____ **D.** teenagers

4. According to the professor, children do not _____ their accents.

_____ **A.** accept

_____ **B.** choose

_____ **C.** hear

_____ **D.** want

5. How does Paul feel about the way Bernd speaks?

_____ **A.** positive

_____ **B.** negative

_____ **C.** neutral

_____ **D.** unsure

6. How does Maria feel about the way teenagers talk today?

_____ **A.** positive

_____ **B.** negative

_____ **C.** neutral

_____ **D.** unsure

**1.3**  CD 1 *Listen to "Code-Switching" from* NorthStar: Listening and Speaking 3, *Unit 4. Use the information from this listening and the listening from Part 1.2 to complete the activity. Check (✔) the boxes where the keywords were associated with* Dialect, Accent, *or* Neither.

| Keyword | Dialect | Accent | Neither |
|---|---|---|---|
| Social status |  |  | ✓ |
| 1. Code-switching |  |  |  |
| 2. Slang |  |  |  |
| 3. Pronunciation |  |  |  |

## PART 2: VOCABULARY

**2.1**  *Read the paragraph. Use the words from the box to fill in the blanks. Not all the words will be used.*

| | | | |
|---|---|---|---|
| cross the line | identity | make a big deal about | stereotype |
| fit in | intentionally | self-conscious | stick up for yourself |

There are some people who are very _____ about the way they
                                                    1.
sound when they speak in another country. However, they should not

_____ this because they can still _____ with the
        2.                                                      3.
people in that country by respecting the traditions and norms. In doing this,

they can still keep their own _____ and don't have to
                                            4.
_____ try to change their accent.
        5.

**2.2**  *Read the statements. Check (✔) the answer that best completes each statement.*

1. To *lay off* something means to _____ doing it.

   _____ **A.** stop              _____ **C.** hate

   _____ **B.** consider          _____ **D.** start

2. To *stereotype* someone means to _____ that person.

   _____ **A.** be mad at         _____ **C.** give support for

   _____ **B.** critically judge  _____ **D.** interrupt

3. A *dialect* is a unique form of _____.

   _____ **A.** an accent         _____ **C.** a language

   _____ **B.** an expression     _____ **D.** slang

4. To *accept* an accent means to _____ that accent.

   _____ **A.** approve of        _____ **C.** reject

   _____ **B.** deny              _____ **D.** speak with

5. To *cross the line* means to _____.

   _____ **A.** act acceptably    _____ **C.** defend yourself

   _____ **B.** behave unacceptably  _____ **D.** take care of a problem

## PART 3:  SKILLS FOR SPEAKING

**3.1**  *Complete the passage.  Fill in the blanks using the correct form of the modals* can, can't, could, *and* couldn't.

When I moved to China, I _____ say anything because I was afraid to speak.
1.

After spending time there, I realized that I _____ learn from others if I just
2.

tried to speak with them. So, I tried to speak with everyone! Now, I _____
3.

speak Chinese quite well, but I still _____ get rid of my accent, and that's okay
4.

with me.

**3.2**  CD 7 (18) *Listen to the sentences.  Circle the modals that you hear.*

Sometimes I can / (can't) understand her accent.

1. I can / can't come to the university tonight.

2. He can / can't speak Spanish.

3. We can / can't wait for you here.

**3.3**  *Read the parts of a classroom discussion.  Circle the sentence or part of the sentence where someone is trying to direct the conversation. You should circle only one sentence or part of a sentence.*

**Getting everyone to speak**

PAUL:        So does that mean parents shouldn't get too hung up about the way their kids speak? Maybe they shouldn't try to correct their children's pronunciation.

PROFESSOR:  Well, that's an interesting point, Paul. (Can we hear from someone else now?)

1. **Starting a discussion**

PROFESSOR:  Today I'd like to discuss what we mean by "accent" in speech. What do we mean when we say "She speaks with an accent"? Maria?

2. **Staying on the topic**

MARIA:       Listen to how teenagers talk today! I can't believe their parents let them use some of those words.

PROFESSOR:  Yes, slang is very interesting, but let's get back to our discussion about accents.

*(continued on next page)*

### 3. Ending a discussion

ANA:       No, I'll never understand all the slang. But my friends tell me not to make a big deal about it. They can't understand half the slang teenagers use either.

PROFESSOR:  This is an interesting discussion, but I'm afraid that's all we have time for today.

## PART 4: SPEAKING

**4.1**  *Say one thing you <u>would do</u> when leading a discussion.*

**4.2**  *Say one thing you <u>would not do</u> when leading a discussion.*

**4.3**  *Leading a Discussion*

*Speak for 1–2 minutes. Explain how you would lead a classroom discussion about language learning.*
- Take notes.
- Use modals of ability and possibility.
- Be sure to pronounce *can* and *can't* correctly.
- Use the vocabulary and grammar from Unit 4.

| **Unit 4 Vocabulary Words** | | | | |
|---|---|---|---|---|
| accept | fit in | intentionally | make a big deal | slang |
| cross the line | get hung up about | lay off | self-conscious | stereotype |
| **Unit 4 Grammar: Modals of Ability and Possibility** | | | | |
| • He *can* come visit us if he's feeling better. | | | | |

# Achievement Tests
# Unit 5

**Name:** _____

**Date:** _____

## PART I: LISTENING

**1.1** CD 7 **19** *Listen to the beginning of a news report about Thailand. Check (✔) the best prediction of what the news report contains. There is only one right answer.*

_____ **A.** information about religious holidays

_____ **B.** information about celebrating elephants

_____ **C.** information about tourist travel

_____ **D.** information about the national flag

**1.2** CD 7 **20** *Now listen to the entire news report. Use the information to choose the correct answers. Check (✔) the answers.*

1. Elephant Day is celebrated on _____ in Thailand.

   _____ **A.** March 13th

   _____ **B.** March 3rd

   _____ **C.** March 30th

   _____ **D.** March 15th

2. In Bangkok, it is against the law to have elephants _____.

   _____ **A.** go hungry

   _____ **B.** be wild

   _____ **C.** beg

   _____ **D.** live freely

3. The tourist's tone of voice suggests that the tourist was _____.

   _____ **A.** accepting

   _____ **B.** sad

   _____ **C.** surprised

   _____ **D.** argumentative

4. Dumbo Express is a group of people that _____.

   _____ **A.** arranges trips to see elephants in the wild

   _____ **B.** helps elephants get medical attention

   _____ **C.** makes sure elephants are not begging

   _____ **D.** gives food to hungry elephants

*(continued on next page)*

5. According to the news report, Thai elephants are _____.

_____ **A.** no longer important to Thai people

_____ **B.** only important to attract tourists

_____ **C.** not safe to live alone in the wild

_____ **D.** in danger of becoming extinct

6. Elephants are celebrated in Thailand because they _____.

_____ **A.** have a long tradition in Thai culture

_____ **B.** are very popular with the tourists

_____ **C.** were once a national symbol

_____ **D.** are helpful for restaurant owners

**1.3** CD7 *Listen to the excerpt from "Tourist Attraction or Human Zoo?" from* NorthStar: Listening and Speaking 3, *Unit 5. Use the information from this listening and the listening from Part 1.2 to complete the activity. Write the letters of the negative statements in the box.*

A. ~~The women care only about earning money.~~

B. It helps preserve one of the greatest Thai traditions.

C. They are causing unnecessary harm to their bodies.

D. They are forced to do degrading things by the restaurant owners.

E. The Thai people benefit from interested tourists.

F. Old traditions are used to carn money.

| Negative Opinions | | |
|---|---|---|
| Pa Daung Tribe | Thai Elephants | Both |
| A<br><br>1. | 2. | 3. |

## PART 2: VOCABULARY

**2.1**  *Match the words and phrases in Column A with their definitions in Column B. Write the letter of the definition on the line. Not all of the definitions will be used.*

| Column A | Column B |
|---|---|
| _____ 1. make a living | **A.** a small town |
| _____ 2. season | **B.** a popular place visited by many people |
| _____ 3. village | **C.** a certain time of the year |
| _____ 4. tourist attraction | **D.** trust in someone to help you |
| _____ 5. depend on | **E.** do something to earn money |
| | **F.** agree on |
| | **G.** people living in a town |

**2.2**  *Check (✔) the meaning of the word.*

1. controversy

   _____ **A.** experience          _____ **C.** disagreement

   _____ **B.** agreement           _____ **D.** understanding

2. stretch (v.)

   _____ **A.** lengthen            _____ **C.** reduce

   _____ **B.** create              _____ **D.** shorten

3. degrading (adj.)

   _____ **A.** disrespectful       _____ **C.** healthy

   _____ **B.** honoring            _____ **D.** exciting

4. souvenir

   _____ **A.** an object you give as a birthday present

   _____ **B.** an object you keep to remember a place

   _____ **C.** an object you win in a game

   _____ **D.** an old object you throw away

5. tradition

   _____ **A.** idea               _____ **C.** treasure

   _____ **B.** circumstance       _____ **D.** custom

## PART 3.  SKILLS FOR SPEAKING

**3.1**  *Complete the sentences using the words in parentheses. Be sure to use* will *when appropriate.*

If tourists do not visit their villages and spend money, the Pa Daung women __will probably not make__ (probably / not / make) enough money for living.

1. Just as the women in their families once did, these women _____ (wrap) brass rings around their necks to stretch them.

2. If the women remove the rings from their necks, they _____ (not / be able to) keep their heads from falling forward because their necks are so weak.

3. Some visitors to the Pa Daung village think that this tradition is unsafe, but almost all the visitors agree that the tradition _____ (continue) as long as there is money to be made.

**3.2**  (CD 7 · 22) *Listen and circle the pronunciation of the* o(s) *in each word.*

so      **A.** [ow] like *go*      **C.** [ɔ] like *law*
     **B.** [a] like *father*      **D.** [ə] like *cut*

1. commerce      **A.** [uw] like *do*      **C.** [a] like *father*
     **B.** [ow] like *go*      **D.** [ʊ] like *could*

2. zoo      **A.** [ʊ] like *could*      **C.** [a] like *father*
     **B.** [ɪw] like *do*      **D.** [ɔ] like *law*

3. book      **A.** [uw] like *do*      **C.** [ə] like *cut*
     **B.** [ʊ] like *could*      **D.** [ow] like *go*

4. sport      **A.** [ɔ] like *law*      **C.** [uw] like *do*
     **B.** [I] like *sit*      **D.** [ow] like *go*

**3.3**  *Complete each sentence with the strongest suggestion.*

We _____should_____ (might want to / should / could) go to Cape Cod tomorrow because the weather report showed that it will be sunny all day.

1. Those people _____ (might not want to / should not / definitely should not) throw their trash into the water because it is not safe for other people at the beach.

2. _____ (Let's / We could / We might want to) take a boat ride around the cape and see all of the beautiful houses along the shore.

3. _____ (We should / We could / We might want to) buy souvenirs today.

## PART 4: SPEAKING

**4.1**  *Write and say a strong suggestion for keeping elephant attractions in Thailand.*

**4.2**  *Write and say a weak suggestion for keeping elephant attractions in Thailand.*

**4.3**  *Making Suggestions*

*Speak for 1–2 minutes from a tourist's point of view. Suggest two possible solutions for a compromise between the animal protection group and the tourist about keeping elephant attractions.*

- Take notes.
- Refer to your suggestions and the animal protection group's suggestions.
- Make future predictions with *if-* clauses.
- Use the vocabulary and grammar from Unit 5.

| **Unit 5 Vocabulary Words** | | | |
|---|---|---|---|
| afford | depend on | season | tourist attraction |
| controversy | make a living | souvenir | tradition |
| degrading | preserve | stretch | village |
| **Unit 5 Grammar:  Future Predictions with *If-* Clauses** | | | |
| • If it keeps raining, the tourists won't come. | | | |

# Achievement Tests
# Unit 6

Name: _____

Date: _____

## PART I: LISTENING

**1.1** CD7 ㉓ *Listen to the beginning of a story. Check (✔) the best prediction of what the listening is about. There is only one right answer.*

_____ **A.** Jim's exciting weekend

_____ **B.** Jim's awful day at work

_____ **C.** Jim's friend Serena

_____ **D.** Jim's scary evening

**1.2** CD7 ㉔ *Now listen to the entire story. Use the information to choose the correct answers. Check (✔) the answers.*

1. Jim appeared to feel _____ because of the voice.

_____ **A.** afraid　　　　　　_____ **C.** lonely

_____ **B.** angry　　　　　　_____ **D.** sad

2. The voice telling Jim to "GO BACK" came from Jim's _____.

_____ **A.** blind date　　　　_____ **C.** mind

_____ **B.** electronics　　　　_____ **D.** workmate

3. Jim was nervous about the blind date because he _____.

_____ **A.** couldn't use his phone　　　_____ **C.** did not want to go

_____ **B.** did not know the person　　　_____ **D.** kept hearing the voice

**1.3** *Read the sentences about the listening passage. Write the numbers 2–4 next to the sentences in the order they happened.*

_____ **A.** The voice told Jim to "GO BACK" when he picked up his phone.

__1__ **B.** Jim heard the voice as he approached his car.

_____ **C.** Jim settled down and began reading his book.

_____ **D.** Jim threw his electronic things into the trash can.

**1.4** 🔊 *Listen to "Lavender" from* NorthStar: Listening and Speaking 3, *Unit 6. Use the information from this listening and the listening from Part 1.2 to complete the activity. Check (✔) the technique that is used in each story.*

| Techniques | "Lavender" | "Go Back" | Both |
|---|---|---|---|
| Uses dialogue | | | ✓ |
| 1. Uses different voices | | | |
| 2. Talks faster and louder | | | |
| 3. Talks slowly and softly | | | |

## PART 2: VOCABULARY

**2.1** *Read the paragraph. Use the words from the box to fill in the blanks. Not all the words will be used.*

| | | | |
|---|---|---|---|
| approaching | driveway | scary | wears on |
| chilled | repeated | technique | whispered |

Ahhh, Friday at last, Jim was thinking.

"Bye, Jim," Serena waved as she walked out the door. "Have a good weekend."

"Can't wait. You, too." Jim was _____ his car when he heard a voice, "Go
                                              **1.**

back," it _____.
            **2.**

Jim looked around, but saw no one. "Huh, I must be working too hard."

Ignoring the voice, he started up his car and drove along the familiar route home.

"Finally. I've been looking forward to this all week," he thought as he turned into

the _____. "Go back," the voice _____.
        **3.**                                **4.**

Now Jim was beginning to worry. "Did I forget something at work? Is that what

'go back' means? Well, I'm already home. No going back now."

Just as Jim picked up his cell phone, he heard the _____ voice. "GO BACK!"
                                                          **5.**

This time the voice almost growled its command.

**2.2**  *Read the vocabulary words. Write the word or phrase from the box that is closest in meaning to each vocabulary word. Not all the words will be used.*

| | | |
|---|---|---|
| expecting others to obey rules | people in a story | frightening |
| friendly event | unattractive plants | people at an event |
| get closer to something | to run after something | |

1. scary: _____

2. weeds: _____

3. social: _____

4. audience: _____

5. strict: _____

# PART 3: SKILLS FOR SPEAKING

**3.1**  *Complete the passage with the correct form of the verbs in parentheses.*

Storytellers often use a variety of techniques _____ a story. Sometimes they
                                                **1. (tell)**

_____ to use different voices. This technique can be effective _____
**2. (try)**                                                                    **3. (scare)**

audiences. However, they also use different voices _____ the story more
                                                    **4. (make)**

exciting.

**3.2**  <sup>C D 7</sup> (26) *Listen to the sentences. Write the preposition that you hear in the blank.*

     Did I forget something ___*at*___ work?

1. Jim had already forgotten _____ the voice.

2. He started up his car and drove _____ the familiar route.

3. The voice screamed _____ the television.

**3.3**  *Read the sentences from a story. Write if they would occur in the beginning (B), middle (M), or end (E) of a story.*

> _____M_____   Just as Jim picked up his cell phone, he heard the scary voice.

> _____ **1.**   Once upon a time there was a man who heard voices coming from his cell phone.

> _____ **2.**   From then on, Jim decided to stop using all of the electronics in his house.

> _____ **3.**   Later that evening, Jim had already forgotten about the voice.

## PART 4: SPEAKING

**4.1**  *Say one emotion that the main character from Part 1.2 <u>did not</u> feel. You may listen again to Part 1.2.*

**4.2**  *Say one way the story would have been different if the main character had not thrown everything into the trash can.*

**4.3**  *Re-telling a Story*

*Speak for 1–2 minutes. Imagine that the main character had not thrown everything into the trash can. Re-tell the story.*
- Take notes.
- Refer to the listening and information from Part 1.2.
- Use various storytelling techniques.
- Use transition words and phrases to give information about the time when events happen in the story.
- Use the vocabulary and grammar from Unit 6.

| Unit 6 Vocabulary Words | | | | | |
|---|---|---|---|---|---|
| approached<br>audience | chilled<br>date | driveway<br>growled | repeated<br>scary | social (n.)<br>strict | weeds<br>whispered |
| **Unit 6 Grammar: Infinitives of Purpose** | | | | | |
| • They use them **to make** their stories good. | | | | | |

# Achievement Tests
# Unit 7

**Name:** _____

**Date:** _____

## PART 1: LISTENING

**1.1** ᶜ ᴰ ⁷ 〈27〉 *Listen to the beginning of a passage. What is being described? Check (✔) the best answer. There is only one right answer.*

_____ **A.** some people's morning routine

_____ **B.** some people's work routine

_____ **C.** some people's favorite coffee

_____ **D.** some people's bad habits

**1.2** ᶜ ᴰ ⁷ 〈28〉 *Now listen to the entire passage. Use the information to choose the correct answers. Check (✔) the answers.*

1. The speaker prefers to _____ in the morning.

_____ **A.** sleep late

_____ **B.** relax a bit

_____ **C.** move quickly

_____ **D.** wake up early

2. The speaker thinks people who rush are _____.

_____ **A.** ashamed

_____ **B.** delightful

_____ **C.** insane

_____ **D.** simple

3. The speaker likes to drink her coffee at the _____ table.

_____ **A.** bedroom

_____ **B.** breakfast

_____ **C.** dining room

_____ **D.** living room

4. The second-hand table was probably bought at a _____.

_____ **A.** department store

_____ **B.** new furniture store

_____ **C.** shopping mall

_____ **D.** used furniture store

5. Coffee that has a rich aroma smells _____.

_____ **A.** burnt

_____ **B.** pleasant

_____ **C.** sweet

_____ **D.** unpleasant

6. The speaker thinks about the day after her _____ cup of coffee.

_____ **A.** first

_____ **B.** second

_____ **C.** third

_____ **D.** fourth

**1.3** 🔊 *Listen to "Urban Homesteaders" from* NorthStar: Listening and Speaking 3, *Unit 7. Use the information from this listening and the listening from Part 1.2 to complete the activity. Write the letters in the box if the statements describe both listenings.*

**A.** Hurry to get things done in the morning

~~**B.** Do things differently from most other people~~

**C.** Try to live simple, stress-free lifestyles

**D.** Get local kids involved in helping the community

**E.** Enjoy doing their daily routines

**F.** Do more work to get things they enjoy having

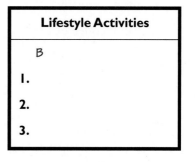

| Lifestyle Activities |
| --- |
| B |
| 1. |
| 2. |
| 3. |

## PART 2: VOCABULARY

**2.1**  *Read the paragraph. Use the words from the box to fill in the blanks. Not all the words will be used.*

| | | | |
|---|---|---|---|
| ashamed | gained | repeated | take it easy |
| convinced | homesteading | simple | worth doing |

I'm not _____ to admit it. I prefer to _____ in the
_____1._____                                    _____2._____

morning. I grind a few spoonfuls of coffee beans and smell their rich aroma. I

continue the process step by step of making a _____ cup of coffee.
_____3._____

This takes a little more time than pushing a button from off to on, but what is lost

in time is _____ in pleasure. The delight of an unhurried morning:
_____4._____

There are those insane people who'll never be _____ .
_____5._____

**2.2**  *Read the analogies. Write whether the analogy describes an Action/Object (A/O), Opposite (O), Description (D), or Part/Whole (P/W) relationship.*

___D___      homesteading: a do-it-yourself lifestyle

_____ **1.** delight: finding joy in something

_____ **2.** self-sufficient: dependent

_____ **3.** insane: sensible

_____ **4.** grind: coffee beans

_____ **5.** flowers: nature

## PART 3: SKILLS FOR SPEAKING

**3.1**  *Read the sentences. Circle the quantifying word or phrase in each sentence.*

(A great deal of) effort is spent making coffee each morning.

1. Before work, many people make coffee for themselves and take it to work.

2. I grind a few spoonfuls of coffee beans and smell their rich aroma.

3. This takes a little more time than pushing a button from off to on.

4. In a lot of cases, I don't even notice the time it takes to make it.

**3.2**  CD 7 30 *Listen to the conversations. Circle the sentence that has faster rhythm in each conversation.*

**A:** I feel so tired tonight.
**B:** (You should have a bit more rest.)

1. **A:** Did you get a lot of sleep last night?
   **B:** Well, I went to bed really late.

2. **A:** Mark looks bad today.
   **B:** He's under a lot of stress.

3. **A:** I'm not feeling well this morning.
   **B:** You need a day off.

**3.3**  *Read the passage. Circle the descriptive adjectives.*

For them, the (hurried) routine never changes:

The alarm clock rings, the coffee-maker starts.

Then it's: Take a quick shower, pour a cup of hot coffee;

Rush to get dressed, have a sip of coffee;

Brief look in the mirror, one more gulp of coffee;

## PART 4: SPEAKING

**4.1**  *Say what the person's simple pleasure is in Part 1.2. You may listen again to Part 1.2.*

**4.2**  *Say how this routine makes her feel.*

**4.3**  *Describing a Simple Pleasure*

*Speak for 1–2 minutes about a simple pleasure that you enjoy doing, either alone or with friends.*

- Take notes. Refer to the listening and information from Part 1.2.
- Use nouns and quantifiers correctly.
- Use adjectives and adverbs, specific information, and words that appeal to the senses.
- Use the vocabulary and grammar from Unit 7.

| Unit 7 Vocabulary Words | | | | |
|---|---|---|---|---|
| ashamed<br>convince | delight<br>gain (v.) | have a blast<br>produce (v.) | self-sufficient<br>simple | take it easy<br>worth doing |
| **Unit 7 Grammar:  Nouns and Quantifiers** | | | | |
| • How *many* questions do you have? | | | | |

# Achievement Tests
# Unit 8

**Name:** _____

**Date:** _____

## PART 1: LISTENING

**1.1** 🎵 CD 7 (31) *Listen to the beginning of a radio show. Check (✔) the best prediction of what the callers will discuss. There is only one right answer.*

_____ **A.** their views of marriage before they got married

_____ **B.** how they deal with problems in their marriage

_____ **C.** their expectations before and during marriage

_____ **D.** how their life changed when they got married

**1.2** 🎵 CD 7 (32) *Now listen to the entire radio show. Use the information to choose the correct answers. Check (✔) the answers.*

1. Amani, the second caller, is calling from _____.

   _____ **A.** New York City

   _____ **B.** San Francisco

   _____ **C.** India

   _____ **D.** Minneapolis

2. Amani thinks a prenuptial agreement would not work in her home country because _____.

   _____ **A.** people do not see marriage as a contract

   _____ **B.** parents decide if their daughter will stay at home or work

   _____ **C.** couples usually do not have problems in their marriage

   _____ **D.** parents arrange marriage for their children

3. Why doesn't the third caller, Toshiyuko, need a prenuptial agreement?

   _____ **A.** He and his wife have a lot in common.

   _____ **B.** Couples who sign an agreement do not trust each other.

   _____ **C.** Before they got married, they decided he will take care of the money.

   _____ **D.** Prenuptial agreements are for people who marry for the second time.

*(continued on next page)*

4. What would Suzanne, the first caller, think about this statement:
"Women who work full time should get help around the house"?

_____ **A.** She would not have an opinion. The statement does not apply to her.

_____ **B.** She would agree. Her husband does not help her.

_____ **C.** She would disagree. Her husband works outside and her job is to work around the house.

_____ **D.** She would agree. She and her husband split the work in the house.

5. Which caller(s) think(s) tradition is a good thing in marriage?

_____ **A.** Amani

_____ **B.** Toshiyuko

_____ **C.** Amani and Toshiyuko

_____ **D.** Amani, Toshiyuko, and Suzanne

**1.3**  CD 7 / 33  *Listen to the excerpt from "Reactions to the Prenuptial Agreement" from* NorthStar: *Listening and Speaking 3, Unit 8. Use the information from this listening and the listening from Part 1.2 to complete the activity. Decide whether the statements are for prenuptial agreements and making a list of expectations, against them, or not mentioned. Check (✔) the correct box.*

| Statements | Prenuptial Agreements and Making a List of Expectations Before Marriage | | |
|---|---|---|---|
| | **For** | **Against** | **Not Mentioned** |
| Spouses should follow traditional cultural roles in marriage. | | ✓ | |
| 1. Raising children should be shared equally. | | | |
| 2. You cannot plan all the details in marriage. | | | |
| 3. Household chores should be shared in marriage. | | | |
| 4. Marriage should be about romance and love. | | | |

**T-38**

## PART 2: VOCABULARY

**2.1** *Read a chat room discussion between two friends. Match the words and phrases in Column A with their definitions in Column B. Write the letter of the definition on the line. Not all of the definitions will be used.*

| | |
|---|---|
| **todlmiller:** | Hey there! |
| **jay85:** | Hey Tod, what's up? |
| **todlmiller:** | Not much. How is the wedding planning going? |
| **jay85:** | Man, it's starting to **bother** me. Sarah's **expectations** are so high. |
| **todlmiller:** | Really? |
| **jay85:** | Yeah. One of her **quirks** is that she wants a fairytale wedding she always dreamed about. |
| **todlmiller:** | What's wrong with that? |
| **jay85:** | Well, nothing, but then most of our talks concern money. We must make a **budget** for everything. Today I went to buy some wedding things without her and she **checked up on** me three times. It's driving me crazy. |
| **todlmiller:** | I see, man. I hope you guys will **work** this **out**. |
| **jay85:** | Me too. |
| **todlmiller:** | I gotta go. |
| **jay85:** | Yep, me too. |

**Column A**

_____ 1. bother

_____ 2. expectation

_____ 3. quirk

_____ 4. budget

_____ 5. check up on

_____ 6. work out

**Column B**

**A.** to be in regard to

**B.** discuss openly

**C.** hope that something will happen

**D.** examine if someone is doing things properly

**E.** a legal agreement

**F.** a plan for how to spend money

**G.** annoy

**H.** find a solution for

**I.** unusual trait

   

**2.2**  *Look at the timeline and the words in the box. Write the words from the box under the correct heading.*

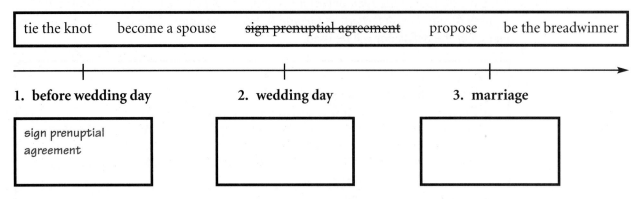

| tie the knot | become a spouse | ~~sign prenuptial agreement~~ | propose | be the breadwinner |

**1.  before wedding day**          **2.  wedding day**          **3.  marriage**

> sign prenuptial
> agreement

## PART 3: SKILLS FOR SPEAKING

**3.1**  *Use the adjectives from the box to fill in the blanks in the letter Tamara has written to her sister. The (+) sign means more. The (–) sign means less. The (=) sign means equal. Not all of the words will be used.*

| adventurous | crowded | free | happy | patient | ~~romantic~~ | windy |

Hawaii, December 10

Dear Sis,

We are enjoying our honeymoon here in Hawaii. It is _____as romantic as_____ I
                                                            (=)

expected. With Steve, I'm _____ I ever
                              1. (+)

was in my life. He makes me laugh all the time!

    The weather is great, and it is _____ they told us it would
                                          2. (–)

be this time of year. There are fewer tourists, so the beaches are

_____ when we were here together. That was a great time,
     3. (–)

remember? But I have to tell you, Steve is _____ you are. We went
                                               4. (+)

surfing this morning! Waves were high, and it was a lot of fun.

Love,
Tamara

**3.2**  CD 7  *Listen to the sentences.  One word in each sentence is emphasized.  Circle the*
        34  *meaning of the sentence.*

(**A.**) Not Ben's
 **B.** Not make the beds
 **C.** Not dry the dishes

 **1.**
 **A.** Not Lynn
 **B.** Not for food
 **C.** Not sometimes

 **2.**
 **A.** Not the bathroom
 **B.** Not the whole house
 **C.** Not his sister

 **3.**
 **A.** Not my daughter
 **B.** Not always
 **C.** Not lunch

**3.3**  *Read the text of an oral presentation.  The transitions for introducing the main idea and
the supporting points are missing.  Write the letter of the correct transition next to the
sentence.*

All of us use the Internet every day for many reasons: to get the news, shop, pay
bills, and play games. But do you know how many young people use the Internet
for dating?

_____B____ Internet dating sites and list main advantages of meeting a love of your
            life online.

**1.** _____ why Internet dating sites are getting so popular is that a lot of single
          people are so busy that they don't have time to meet other singles in a
          traditional way. That is by far the most common answer you will get from
          a lot of young, single people.

**2.** _____ that people like to spend time on the Internet so it is easy for them to find
          their first date online. And there is one more.

**3.** _____ that you answer many questions when you sign up so you are matched
          with people who are like you.

   **A.** A final reason is                    **D.** Another important reason is

   **B.** Today I'd like to talk about         **E.** The question that I will discuss today is

   **C.** One reason is                        **F.** The most important reason

## PART 4: SPEAKING

**4.1**  *Imagine that you agree with Suzanne from Part 1.2. Say a reason why you support what she is saying. You may listen again to Part 1.2.*

**4.2**  *Now imagine that you agree with Amani. Say a reason why you support what she is saying.*

**4.3**  *Presenting Both Sides of an Issue*

*Speak for 1–2 minutes. Present both views to the class. State Suzanne and Amani's opinions about writing down your expectations before getting married. Then give your opinions. Support your opinions with examples. Make a concluding sentence.*

- Take notes.
- Use comparatives and equatives.
- Emphasize words that show a contrast.
- Use transitions for introducing main ideas and supporting points.
- Use the vocabulary and grammar from Unit 8.

| Unit 8 Vocabulary Words | | | |
| --- | --- | --- | --- |
| bother | check up on | expectation | quirk |
| breadwinner | concern | occur | tie the knot |
| budget | contract | open up | work out |

| Unit 8 Grammar: Comparatives and Equatives |
| --- |
| • Anna is **as tall as** Jim. <br> • Jim is **taller than** Arvind. <br> • Your job is **more difficult than** my job. <br> • My homework is **less difficult than** your homework. |

# Achievement Tests
# Unit 9

Name: _____

Date: _____

## PART I: LISTENING

**1.1** CD7 (35) *Listen to the beginning of a speech from an environmental rally. Check (✔) the best prediction of what the speech will be about. There is only one right answer.*

_____ **A.** the greenhouse effect

_____ **B.** global warming

_____ **C.** ways to help the environment

_____ **D.** businesses' effects on the atmosphere

**1.2** CD7 (36) *Now listen to the entire speech. Use the information to choose the correct answers. Check (✔) whether the statements are true (T), false (F), or not mentioned in the speech.*

1. The man talks about what businesses can do to protect the environment.

   _____ T        _____ F        _____ not mentioned

2. The new law will cover the period of five years.

   _____ T        _____ F        _____ not mentioned

3. Big businesses have greater responsibility than individuals in reducing the carbon footprint.

   _____ T        _____ F        _____ not mentioned

4. During summer months, turning the air conditioner down can help.

   _____ T        _____ F        _____ not mentioned

5. Using public transportation is one of the alternatives to driving to work.

   _____ T        _____ F        _____ not mentioned

**1.3**  CD 7  *Listen to the excerpt from "A Call to Action" from* NorthStar:  Listening and
         37   *Speaking 3, Unit 9.  Use the information from this listening and the listening from
              Part 1.2 to complete the activity.  Check (✔) the suggestion(s) both speakers
              mentioned.*

| Suggestion | Mentioned by Both Speakers |
|---|---|
| 1.  Emission of gases needs to decrease. | |
| 2.  People should reuse materials such as plastic and metal. | |
| 3.  Energy-saving trucks and cars need to be made. | |
| 4.  People should use public transportation more. | |

## PART 2: VOCABULARY

**2.1**   *Use the words from the box to fill in the blanks.  Not all the words will be used.*

| | | | |
|---|---|---|---|
| challenging | fossil fuels | guilty | invisible |
| emissions | greenhouse gases | individuals | significant |

1.  Two of the major sources of $CO_2$ _____ in our atmosphere are
    factories and businesses.

2.  To help find a solution for global warming, _____ changes in
    people's behavior are necessary.

3.  Carbon dioxide is a(n) _____ gas but in large amounts it
    represents one of the greatest dangers facing the Earth today.

4.  If you do something about reducing your carbon footprint now, you will not
    feel _____ later.

5.  Our planet is getting warmer and warmer because of the _____
    that are trapped in the atmosphere.

**2.2**  *Read the sentences.  Circle the synonym or definition for each underlined word.*

1.  This law would require businesses to reduce the amount of greenhouse gases they <u>emit</u> by a significant amount over the next ten years.

    **A.**  care for

    **B.**  reduce

    **C.**  send out

    **D.**  decrease

2.  Therefore, it is up to each individual to <u>contribute</u> to a cleaner and healthier environment.

    **A.**  help make happen

    **B.**  wonder about

    **C.**  be responsible for

    **D.**  make sure

3.  But you might wonder, "how can I have an <u>impact</u>?".

    **A.**  influence

    **B.**  part

    **C.**  place

    **D.**  crash

4.  We are all <u>guilty</u> of this crime against the environment.

    **A.**  helpful

    **B.**  ashamed

    **C.**  hurtful

    **D.**  healthy

5.  What can I do to <u>offset</u> the dangers that these invisible gases cause?

    **A.**  make someone aware of

    **B.**  stop completely

    **C.**  influence strongly

    **D.**  have the opposite effect on

## PART 3: SKILLS FOR SPEAKING

**3.1**  *Read the interview with a presidential candidate.  Circle the best modal of necessity.*

| | |
|---|---|
| HOST: | Here we are today with Senator Smith, who is running for president in the next year's election. Welcome to the show, Senator Smith. |
| PRES. CANDIDATE: | Thanks for inviting me. |
| HOST: | Senator Smith, if you get elected, what are you going to do about the protection of the environment? |
| PRES. CANDIDATE: | Environmental protection is very important to me and it <u>can't be / will have to be /(must be)</u> for everyone in this country. Why? Because we (1) <u>must not / have to / must</u> waste our time any more. We (2) <u>can't / have to / must</u> depend on fossil fuels any longer. For example, in the next couple of years we (3) <u>will have to / can't / don't have to</u> start using new kinds of fuels such as biofuels. |
| HOST: | Now, some of our viewers may ask: how much is making biofuels going to cost? |
| PRES. CANDIDATE: | It (4) <u>can't / doesn't have to / has to</u> cost a lot. We already have a lot of factories built, and the government will help pay for these programs. |
| HOST: | So, are you are saying that new taxes (5) <u>have to / must / don't have to</u> be introduced to pay for this? |
| PRES. CANDIDATE: | That is right. We do not want new taxes. |
| HOST: | Moving on to the next question . . . |

**3.2**  (CD 7 38) *Listen to the sentences.  Is the speaker finished or not?  Check (✔) the correct box.*

| Sentence | Speaker is finished. | Speaker is not finished. |
|---|---|---|
| I'm going to buy a hybrid car | ✓ | |
| 1. I'm trying to recycle old batteries | | |
| 2. I always turn off the air conditioning when I leave the house | | |
| 3. I'm going to walk to work once a week | | |
| 4. I never leave the lights on when I go to sleep | | |
| 5. I'm not going to throw away glass bottles and cans | | |

## PART 4: SPEAKING

**4.1**  *Explain the term "carbon footprint." You may listen again to Part 1.2.*

**4.2**  *Think about a suggestion the speaker <u>did not</u> mention. Say your suggestion using must not.*

**4.3**  *Helping the Environment*

*Speak for 1–2 minutes. Give your own suggestions for how individuals, industries, or governments can help the environment. Tell your classmates that they can interrupt you politely to ask questions.*

- Give at least two suggestions.
- Use modals of necessity.
- Use proper intonation to indicate that you have more to say or are finished speaking.
- Use the vocabulary and grammar from Unit 9.

| Unit 9 Vocabulary Words | | | | | |
|---|---|---|---|---|---|
| atmosphere<br>challenging | contribute<br>emission | greenhouse gases<br>guilty | impact<br>individual | invisible<br>offset | significant<br>ton |

| Unit 9 Grammar: Modals of Necessity |
|---|
| • You **must** go to class tomorrow.<br>• I **have to** go to class.<br>• You **don't have to** go to the party.<br>• I **must not** be late. |

# Achievement Tests
# Unit 10

**Name:** _____

**Date:** _____

## PART 1: LISTENING

**1.1** 🔘 *Listen to the beginning of a report on a court's decision. Check (✔) the best prediction of what the report is about. There is only one right answer.*

_____ **A.** whether stealing is a crime

_____ **B.** whether a child is responsible for his or her misbehavior

_____ **C.** how parents should discipline their children

_____ **D.** how courts make judgments

**1.2** 🔘 *Now listen to the entire report. Use the information to choose the correct answers. Check (✔) the answers.*

1. The reporter says that _____.

   _____ **A.** people are wondering if Jessica is a thief

   _____ **B.** it is the first time Jessica has been charged with a crime

   _____ **C.** Jessica has been arrested for stealing before

   _____ **D.** Jessica's parents are at the scene of the crime

2. Jessica is _____ years old.

   _____ **A.** 20

   _____ **B.** 6

   _____ **C.** 12

   _____ **D.** 16

3. The elderly man _____ the Court's decision.

   _____ **A.** has not heard about

   _____ **B.** supports

   _____ **C.** opposes

   _____ **D.** does not care about

4. The Jones Center for Family Causes _____.

   _____ **A.** teaches kids to behave

   _____ **B.** punishes children who misbehave

   _____ **C.** helps parents deal with family issues

   _____ **D.** tells courts how to make decisions

5. The woman from the Jones Center for Family Causes believes that

_____ are responsible for children's behavior.

_____ **A.** children

_____ **B.** both children and parents

_____ **C.** governments

_____ **D.** people at the Jones Center

6. The reporter concludes that _____.

_____ **A.** people cannot agree if parents should be punished

_____ **B.** everyone believes that parents are to blame

_____ **C.** parents and children's actions are controversial

_____ **D.** the Court has made a mistake

**1.3**  CD 7 (41) *Listen to the excerpt from "The Spanking Debate" from* NorthStar: Listening and Speaking 3, *Unit 10. Use the information from this listening and the listening from Part 1.2 to complete the activity. Check the box that shows where you heard each suggestion.*

| Suggestion | Both Listenings | Report about Jessica | Interview with Dr. Lau | Neither Listening |
|---|---|---|---|---|
| Limit time in front of TV | | | | ✓ |
| **1.** Spank children occasionally | | | | |
| **2.** Set clear limits | | | | |
| **3.** Teach problem-solving skills | | | | |

## PART 2: VOCABULARY

**2.1**  *Read a letter to a newspaper. Match the words and phrases in Column A with their definitions in Column B. Write the letter of the definition on the line. Not all the definitions will be used.*

---

Dear Abby,

My husband and I need your help with this issue. We have a ten-year-old son, Sam. We are really trying to be good parents, but a lot of our friends tell us we are too **permissive**. For example, Sam is very energetic, and I let him go skateboarding with his friends, but he often **gets carried away**, forgets about the time, and comes home later than he says he will.

My friends tell me I have to **set limits** and show my son there are **consequences** for his **misbehavior**. My mom even tells me I cannot **discipline** my child well and **recommends** that my husband and I talk to a family counselor who can help us all.

Are we bad parents?

Thanks,
Sarah

---

|   Column A   |   Column B   |
|--------------|--------------|
| _____ 1. permissive | **A.** results of an action |
| _____ 2. get carried away | **B.** advise what to do |
| _____ 3. set limits | **C.** very tolerant, allowing a lot of freedom |
| _____ 4. consequences | **D.** problem or concern |
| _____ 5. misbehavior | **E.** feel very excited and behave unreasonably |
| _____ 6. discipline | **F.** remove limitations |
| _____ 7. recommend | **G.** punish |
|  | **H.** negative behavior |
|  | **I.** not acceptable |
|  | **J.** make clear rules for what someone is allowed to do |

**2.2**  *Read the sentences. Circle the synonym for each underlined word.*

1. Many people think that spanking is a form of child <u>abuse</u> and should not be allowed by law.

   **A.** behavior

   **B.** training

   **C.** mistreatment

   **D.** control

2. They <u>advocate</u> that all people take action and call the police if they see or hear about parents using corporal punishment.

   **A.** suggest

   **B.** believe

   **C.** say

   **D.** agree

3. Calling the police may be a <u>short-term</u> solution but can help parents see that they have gone too far.

   **A.** lasting

   **B.** wrong

   **C.** necessary

   **D.** temporary

# PART 3: SKILLS FOR SPEAKING

**3.1**  *Use the verbs in the box to complete the phone conversation. Write the correct form of present perfect.*

| ~~be~~ | buy | listen | read | return | see | spank |
|---|---|---|---|---|---|---|

LARA: Hey Kim, where ___*have*___ you ___*been*___? I tried to call you at least three times.

KIM: I _____ just _____ from a lecture on parenting practices.
                          1.

*(continued on next page)*

LARA: Really? That sounds interesting.

KIM: It was interesting. The professor talked about changes in disciplining children. There is no doubt that spanking is getting less popular.

LARA: That doesn't surprise me. I _____ not _____ any of my friends
2.
spank their children.

KIM: Well, your friends aren't typical. _____ you _____ today newspaper's
3.
cover story? Obviously, more than 90% of parents admit they _____
4.
their kids at least once.

LARA: I can't believe it! That many? Which newspaper was that?

KIM: *The Morning Star.* Anyway, why are you calling?

**3.2**  CD 7  *Listen to each sentence. One word from each sentence will be repeated. Decide*
42  *whether the word ends with the sound /z/, which is voiced, or sound /s/, which is voiceless. Then check (✔) the correct column.*

| Word from Sentence | /z/ | /s/ |
|---|---|---|
| Abuse | | ✓ |
| 1. Advice | | |
| 2. Raise | | |
| 3. Use | | |
| 4. Loose | | |

**3.3**  *Read the sentences. Check (✔) the sentence that is expressing <u>less confidence</u>.*

    1. **KIM:**  <u>There is no doubt</u> that spanking is getting less popular.

       \_\_\_\_\_ **A.**  We know for a fact that spanking is getting less popular.

       \_\_\_\_\_ **B.**  Clearly, spanking is getting less popular.

       \_\_\_\_\_ **C.**  Generally, spanking is getting less popular.

    2. **KIM:**  <u>Obviously,</u> more than 90 percent of parents admit doing that.

       \_\_\_\_\_ **A.**  It is clear that more than 90 percent of parents admit doing that.

       \_\_\_\_\_ **B.**  You could say that more than 90 percent of parents admit doing that.

       \_\_\_\_\_ **C.**  There is no doubt that more than 90 percent of parents admit doing that.

## PART 4: SPEAKING

**4.1**  *Say whether you agree or disagree with the Court's decision in Part 1.2. You may listen again to Part 1.2.*

**4.2**  *Give two reasons to support your opinion using expressions of confidence.*

**4.3**  *Dealing with Misbehavior*

*Speak for 1–2 minutes. Imagine you work for the Jones Center for Family Causes. This center helps parents and children deal with family problems. Talk to a parent who came to the center about how to deal with the problematic behavior (stealing) of her child.*

- Take notes.
- Use the present perfect tense.
- Be sure to pronounce final /s/ and /z/ properly.
- Use expressions of confidence.
- Use the vocabulary and grammar from Unit 10.

| Unit 10 Vocabulary Words | | | | |
|---|---|---|---|---|
| advocate | discipline | misbehavior | problem solving | set limits |
| consequences | get carried away | permissive | recommend | |
| **Unit 10 Grammar: Present Perfect Tense** | | | | |
| • I **have listened** to that song five times today. | | | | |

# Achievement Tests Audioscript

## UNIT 1

### 1.1

**First Man's voice:** Jim, good to see you. This is my wife, Carol.

**Second Man's voice:** Nice to meet you, Carol. And this is my wife, uh . . . uh . . .

**Announcer:** Do you have trouble remembering things? You can't remember where you put your keys, your watch, or even the glasses on top of your head?

### 1.2

**First Man's voice:** Jim, good to see you. This is my wife, Carol.

**Second Man's voice:** Nice to meet you, Carol. And this is my wife, uh . . . uh . . .

**Announcer:** Do you have trouble remembering things? You can't remember where you put your keys, your watch, or even the glasses on top of your head?

Now there's a solution. This little pill called *Don't Forget*. It's so effective you'll never suffer the embarrassment that Jim did.

Look at Jim now, after a week of *Don't Forget*. He's at a party, he's shaking hands with his boss, and with no fear, he's introducing his wife, Elena.

Still not convinced? Listen to what another consumer says about this amazing product.

**Woman's voice:** I just can't emphasize enough how this pill has changed my life. I have four kids and before I took this pill, I couldn't even remember their names!

**Announcer:** Why rely on your memory when you can take this safe, affordable little pill? It's made from all natural ingredients so you don't have to worry about any negative (side) effects. And it costs just pennies a day. *Don't Forget*. It's the one thing you'll always remember.

### 1.3

**Man:** Hey, boy. Come here!

**Dog:** [whines]

**Man:** Hey, what's the matter?

**Dog:** What's the matter? It's the dog food he's feeding me. It's terrible! Woof!! But Spot, in the next yard . . . he gets *Doggie Delight* dog food. Just look at it . . . delicious chunks of meat, tasty vegetables, all covered in creamy gravy! Please, please, I want *Doggie Delight*—wooooo!

**Announcer:** Treat your dog right—get *Doggie Delight!*

## UNIT 2

### 1.1

**Recording:** Thank you for calling the IdentiTrue information line. We are here to help you understand, prevent, and deal with identity theft. To report a crime, you should contact your local police department immediately. If you have been the victim of theft and need advice, please leave a message after the tone. Include your name, contact information, and the details of your situation. We will call back shortly to confirm your information and help you with your problem.

### 1.2

**Recording:** Thank you for calling the IdentiTrue information line. We are here to help you understand, prevent, and deal with identity theft. To report a crime, you should contact your local police department immediately. If you have been the victim of theft and need advice, please leave a message after the tone. Include your name, contact information, and the details of your situation. We will call back shortly to confirm your information and help you with your problem.

**Greta:** Hello? Um, yes, this is Greta Thayer, and I'm calling about a stolen purse. Well, I mean, I left my purse in my car last night and, um, it's still here, but someone totally cleaned it out. Everything is gone—my ID card, my credit cards, my checkbook, even my library card! Who would take a library card?! Plus, I just got a call from Bella's department store, and someone already made a credit card purchase there that I didn't authorize. It turns out this person bought five hundred dollars worth of baby clothes in my name, and I don't even have kids. What a joke! So, I filed a complaint with the police department this morning. They're trying to track down whoever is using my identity, but they said I ought to talk to you about how to protect myself. Please call me back right away. I don't know what to do, and I'm really paranoid about what else might happen. Um, the thief took my cell phone too, but you can call me at home. My number is 555-9056 . . .

### 1.3

**Lily:** So, I was at the computer and the phone rang, I got this phone call, and she said "Well, we have here that you've bought a diamond ring, so I'm just confirming the purchase because it's quite a bit of money." And I said, "Well, what is it?" And she said, "It's a five thousand dollar diamond ring." And I said, "No, I haven't left the house today, so I wouldn't have bought a diamond ring, and anyway, I don't go to that store, I don't go to your store anymore." And so, she said, "Well, somebody who has your name has purchased a diamond ring for five thousand dollars." And I said, "Five thousand dollars! A diamond ring! Well, that's not me. I didn't buy it, and I don't authorize the purchase of this diamond ring, OK? So, we have a problem."

# UNIT 3

## 1.1

You see, several years ago I was in a very difficult stage of life. Two loved ones had recently passed away, and two of my children were fighting a terrible disease. I felt like life had really thrown me for a loop, and some days I was so sad and tired that it was a challenge just to get off the couch. This was not the course I wanted my life to take, but what could I do? Well, one day I just started walking. That's right—*walking*!

## 1.2

Good afternoon, everyone, and thank you for inviting me to your meeting today. I'm here to share what I've learned about setting goals and making your dreams come true. This is easier said than done, of course, but my favorite saying is "You can soar on the wings of an optimistic attitude." Life has taught me that this is true—with a good attitude you really can achieve great things.

You see, several years ago I was in a very difficult stage of life. Two loved ones had recently passed away, and two of my children were fighting a terrible disease. I felt like life had really thrown me for a loop, and some days I was so sad and tired that it was a challenge just to get off the couch. This was not the course I wanted my life to take, but what could I do? Well, one day I just started walking. That's right—*walking*!

That first day I made it a whole ten minutes. Still, I reminded myself of that little saying about soaring on wings—"You can soar on the wings of an optimistic attitude"—and I decided to keep trying. The next day I went a little farther, and the next day farther still. Soon my endurance improved, and I felt so good—mentally and physically—that I even began running.

In just over a year, I lost 100 pounds and achieved a dream that I had set my heart on long ago: I completed a marathon! For each mile of hot mountain terrain, I kept myself going by thinking of a different person who had helped me reach my goal of running the race. I think having them with me through those twenty-six miles helped me finish.

My desire to live a full, healthy life had been my motivation for running. After reaching that goal, I wanted to help others, so I wrote a book about my experience and helped to organize a yearly race to raise money for women's health. It's hard to believe that just a few years ago I could hardly walk down the street, because now I feel wonderful. I just hope my story can inspire others—maybe even some of you—to keep a positive attitude and help yourselves in the same way.

## 1.3

**Tim Bourquin:** Well, you know Jay, it doesn't sound like a whole lot of fun, so, you know, in the night, you're not getting a lot of sleep. What is in it for you? What does the race do for you personally?

**Jay Batchen:** That's a good question, and it's a question that many people ask. And what I tell them is that this race is more than a race. It's a life experience. And what I mean by that is: you're sharing a tent with eight other people, and you're going through the same highs and lows every day. It might not be at the same time, but you're running in the same heat, you're running in the same wind, you're sleeping in the same sandstorms on the cold nights, and for me it's about meeting the other people that are running this event, and sharing stories with them and sharing the experience with them. And it's so hard to describe to someone who hasn't been there and run the event. So for me, it's completing the distance and knowing that I can do it, feeling that I can do it, but it's meeting the people from all over the world, from all walks of life, and just sharing it with them that makes it special.

## 3.2

He ate <u>something or other</u> and felt sick.

1. We went to a great party <u>the other night</u>.
2. They argue with <u>each other</u> all the time.
3. I want to live alone. I don't want <u>another</u> roommate.

# UNIT 4

## 1.1

**Professor:** Today I'd like to discuss what we mean by "accent" in speech. What do we mean when we say "She speaks with an accent"? Maria?

## 1.2

**Professor:** Today I'd like to discuss what we mean by "accent" in speech. What do we mean when we say "She speaks with an accent"? Maria?

**Maria:** Doesn't that mean the way we sound when we speak?

**Professor:** Yes, that's right. An accent refers to a person's pronunciation.

Remember, it's not the same as a dialect.

So, your assignment was to interview three people about their accents.

Today let's hear about one of the people you interviewed.

**Paul:** I was talking to my friend, Bernd. His parents came from Germany about 30 years ago. I don't want to make a big deal of it, but they both sound like they just came to the United States. It seems so weird because when Bernd was a baby, he obviously learned to speak from his parents. So why doesn't Bernd have a German accent? He talks just like I do.

**Professor:** You've brought up an interesting point. It has a lot to do with how important it is for children to separate from their parents and develop their own identities. Children naturally want to fit in with kids of their age group. To be accepted by them, they have to dress like their friends, talk like they do, maybe even like the same movies they do.

**Paul:** But not all kids want to be like everyone else. Don't they have a choice?

**Professor:** Sure. In some ways they do. For example, they can dress the way they want to, but when it comes to the way they talk, it appears that they don't intentionally make a decision about their accent.

**Paul:** So does that mean parents shouldn't get too hung up about the way their kids speak? Maybe they shouldn't try to correct their children's pronunciation.

**Professor:** Well, that's an interesting point, Paul. Can we hear from someone else now?

**Maria:** I was wondering about how kids learn slang? It seems like they make a lot of decisions about what slang words to use. Especially teenagers. If a word is cool one day, they immediately decide to use that word so they won't be stereotyped as "uncool." Listen to how teenagers talk today! I can't believe their parents let them use some of those words.

**Professor:** Yes, slang is very interesting, but let's get back to our discussion about accents...

### 1.3

**Professor:** So, let's get back to this idea of code-switching, which I mentioned earlier. Code-switching is when a person switches—changes—from one language or dialect to another. So someone may speak one way at work or school, but another way at home or with friends. Basically they switch languages or dialects depending on where they are and who they're talking to.

One example of code-switching—changing dialects—is the way teenagers change their speech when talking to their friends versus talking to an adult. A lot of teenagers speak a "teen dialect," which is a dialect used by teenagers with a lot of slang ... slang their parents don't understand and usually hate too, right? Like they're saying "Why are you talking like that? What are you saying?"

But when kids switch between this teen dialect and the standard dialect, this is code-switching. So, let me give you an example. Let's say a teenager is leaving the house and he says to his friend, "Gotta bounce. We gotta meet the crew." Then his dad asks, "Hey, where're you going?" and the kid says, "We have to go. We're meeting our friends dowtown." So he's saying the same thing to both people, but with his friends using a teen dialect, "Gotta bounce" meaning "We have to go" and "the crew" for "my friends." And he's code-switching when he switches from the teen dialect into standard English with his dad.

Alright, so why do teenagers use this kind of teen dialect? Well, because it's an important way for teens to show their identity—to show that they fit in with their friends. It also shows that they're separate from their parents. So by code-switching into a teen dialect with their friends, a teen is saying, "I'm one of you." ... and saying to their parents, "I'm *not* like *you.*"

### 3.2

Sometimes I <u>can't</u> understand her accent.
1. I <u>can</u> come to the university tonight.
2. He <u>can't</u> speak Spanish.
3. We <u>can't</u> wait for you here.

## UNIT 5

### 1.1

**Susan Cormal:** One might wonder—why celebrate a holiday in honor of the elephant? Well, the elephant has a long tradition in Thai culture. At one time, the Thai depended on elephants to fight in wars alongside them. Elephants also played a role in religious ceremonies. These are some of the reasons the Thai have such a love for the elephant and have included it on the national flag of Thailand.

### 1.2

**Anchor:** It's March 13th and in Thailand people are celebrating a tradition called Elephant Day. With the elephant facing extinction, what does this mean for the survival of this holiday? Susan Cormal reports.

**Susan Cormal:** One might wonder—why celebrate a holiday in honor of the elephant? Well, the elephant has a long tradition in Thai culture. At one time, the Thai depended on elephants to fight in wars alongside them. Elephants also played a role in religious ceremonies. These are some of the reasons the Thai have such a love for the elephant and have included it on the national flag of Thailand.

Unfortunately, the beloved elephant may become extinct. Instead of living freely in the wild, the elephant today is usually used to help restaurant owners make a living. I'm now standing outside a restaurant in Bangkok, the capital of Thailand. A young woman is stretching out her hand to feed a hungry elephant. "Begging" elephants are a common tourist attraction in Bangkok, even though there is a city law against it.

Let me find out if this young woman is aware of the law. Excuse me, I'm here reporting about Elephant Day. Can I ask you a question?

**Tourist:** Sure. I'll have some amazing stories to tell when I go back home. In fact, would you take a picture of me feeding an elephant?

**Susan Cormal:** Did you know that many people believe this is degrading to elephants? There's even a law against using elephants to beg in the streets.

**Tourist:** Oh no! I had no idea. I think the guidebooks should definitely mention this. Most books only tell you which season is the best time to travel, what hotels you can or can't afford, and where you can find the best souvenirs.

**Susan Cormal:** Now I'd like to talk to someone who knows more about the problem of the elephant than almost anyone. Sang Tounserat has founded Dumbo Express, a group of veterinarians who seek out elephants in need of medical attention.

So is Elephant Day a sad day for you? A time when people are celebrating a national treasure that may soon be extinct?

**Sang Tounserat:** Really, I think it's the best time to make people aware of this controversy. I like to use this day to educate the public and let them know how Dumbo Express helps. You can make a contribution just by visiting the park. Or if you'd like, you can shop online at dumboexpress.com.

**Susan Cormal:** It's a sad day when the national symbol of a country may soon be extinct. But with people like Sang, and her work at Dumbo Express, there's now much more to celebrate on Elephant Day.

This is Susan Cormal, in Bangkok, Thailand.

## 1.3

**Frederick:** Actually, I don't see that we're preserving tradition at all. This tradition has died in Myanmar already. These women are just hurting their bodies to entertain us. It's like paying to go see animals in a zoo. It's degrading.

# UNIT 6

## 1.1

Ahhh, Friday at last, Jim was thinking.

"Bye, Jim," Serena waved as she walked out the door. "Have a good weekend."

"Can't wait. You, too." Jim was approaching his car when he heard a voice, "Go back," it whispered.

Jim looked around, but saw no one. "Huh, I must be working too hard." Ignoring the voice, he started up his car and drove along the familiar route home.

"Finally. I've been looking forward to this all week," he thought as he turned into the driveway. "Go back," the voice repeated.

## 1.2

Ahhh, Friday at last, Jim was thinking.

"Bye, Jim," Serena waved as she walked out the door. "Have a good weekend."

"Can't wait. You, too." Jim was approaching his car when he heard a voice, "Go back," it whispered.

Jim looked around, but saw no one. "Huh, I must be working too hard." Ignoring the voice, he started up his car and drove along the familiar route home.

"Finally. I've been looking forward to this all week," he thought as he turned into the driveway. "Go back," the voice repeated.

Now Jim was beginning to worry. "Did I forget something at work? Is that what 'go back' means? Well, I'm already home. No going back now."

Later that evening, Jim had already forgotten about the voice. He was thinking about the blind date he would have on Saturday night. Jim was a little nervous, but also excited at the thought of meeting someone new. He thought he would call his friend John, who had arranged the date.

Just as Jim picked up his cell phone, he heard the scary voice. "GO BACK!" This time the voice almost growled its command.

To get the voice out of his mind, he slipped a DVD into the player and began to watch a movie.

"GO BACK!" the voice screamed from the television.

"I can't stand this!" Jim yelled as he turned off the DVD player.

"GO BACK!" This time the voice came from his laptop. "GO BACK!" Now his computer was giving him the same message.

Jim was desperate. He gathered his cell phone, DVD player, laptop, even the iPod he had bought only days before and threw them into the trash can.

Suddenly, it was quiet. The voice was gone. Jim picked up a book he had started a month ago and began to read.

"Aha!" he said. It finally made sense. It was as if Jim had gone back in time 30 years, before the world depended on the latest technological invention to do something as simple as enjoy a relaxing weekend.

## 1.4

Robert and David were good friends. Late one spring evening, they were driving to a spring social. As they drove along the road, Robert and David both realized that they didn't have dates! So David said to Robert, "Some good friend you are. What happened to our dates for the evening?"

"Oh, I'm sorry. I just couldn't get them to go."

"Well, we'll find dates at the dance. There'll be lots of girls there without partners."

As they drove along the road, the headlights fell on someone walking along the side of the highway. As they approached the person walking, they could see that it was a young girl, dressed in a lavender evening dress. Robert looked at David, David looked at Robert, and they both smiled. They slowed the car down, and when they stopped, they said to the young woman, "We're on our way to the social."

"Oh," she said, "so am I!"

"Would you like to ride?"

"I would indeed," she said.

She got into the back of the car. Robert and David introduced themselves and she said, "I'm Lavender, just like my dress. Just call me Lavender."

As they drove along, they decided that they would be together that night. At the dance, Robert danced with Lavender, David danced with Lavender, and as the evening wore on, the spring air turned a little cool. And Robert said to Lavender, "Are you cold? Would you like my coat?"

"Oh, yes," she said, "I am just a bit chilled."

And Robert said, "I think it's raining outside. Could we drive you home?"

"Oh, yes," she said, "Thank you. I didn't want to walk on the highway alone tonight."

And as they started down the highway, Lavender explained that both her mom and dad were just a little strict. And it would be very difficult to explain how she had come home with two strange young men. So it would be easier to stop at the edge of the driveway and she could walk to the house without any explanation to her parents. And Robert and David understood. And as they stopped at the edge of the driveway, Lavender got out, blew them a kiss from the tip of her fingers, and walked down the driveway and through the trees toward the house. And then they realized that she still had the coat! David said, "Tomorrow. We'll get it back tomorrow. That will be the excuse we use to come and visit."

Early the next morning, David and Robert were on the highway, driving toward the house. But as they drove up and down the highway, they couldn't seem to find the driveway.

"It was here!"

"No, it was over there!"

"It was here," said Robert, "but look, it's all grown up. There are weeds, and grass, and rocks. It wasn't grown up last night! But this is the driveway . . . you see, there's a house between the trees."

So they stopped the car and got out, and walked along the driveway. And as they cleared the trees, they could see the house. And Robert said to David, "Are you sure that we're in the right place? Look at this house. Look at the windows—they're all broken! And look how the door hangs from the hinges! This couldn't be the place!" They walked to the back of the house. And there, in a little picket fence, was a little family cemetery with five, six, seven gravestones. And hanging on one of the gravestones, a middle-sized gravestone, was the coat. And as they lifted the coat from the stone they both said, "Aaah!"

The name on the gravestone was "Lavender." They spent the evening with a ghost. And that's the end of that!

## 3.2

Did I forget something <u>at</u> work?
1. Jim had already forgotten <u>about</u> the voice.
2. He started up his car and drove <u>along</u> the familiar route.
3. The voice screamed <u>from</u> the television.

# UNIT 7

## 1.1

There are those insane people who have the coffee-maker set to go as soon as the alarm clock rings. For them, the hurried routine never changes:

The alarm clock rings, the coffee-maker starts. Then it's:
Take a quick shower, pour a cup of coffee;
Rush to get dressed, have a sip of coffee . . .

## 1.2

There are those insane people who have the coffee-maker set to go as soon as the alarm clock rings. For them, the hurried routine never changes:

The alarm clock rings, the coffee-maker starts. Then it's:
Take a quick shower, pour a cup of coffee;
Rush to get dressed, have a sip of coffee;
Brief look in the mirror, one more gulp of coffee;
Then briefcase in hand, last swallow of coffee, they dash out the door and run off to work.

I'm not ashamed to admit it. I prefer to take it easy in the morning. My eyes open and I slowly unfold with a stretch. Then my feet touch the floor and I move leisurely to the kitchen. Now my morning ritual begins. I grind a few spoonfuls of coffee beans and smell their rich aroma. I continue the process step by step of making a simple cup of coffee. This takes a little more time than pushing a button from off to on, but what is lost in time is gained in pleasure.

The ritual continues as I take my steaming cup of coffee and set it on the dining room table. Seated at this second-hand table, I enjoy my first sip of coffee while I gaze out the window. I have another sip and read the morning paper. It's only after I've finished the second cup of coffee that I begin to think about the day ahead.

The delight of an unhurried morning: There are those insane people who'll never be convinced.

## 1.3

**Karen Brown:** A group of chickens are walking around the backyard of Daniel Staub, Kristin Brennan, and their two young children. The chickens lay about ten eggs a day. In their garden, vegetables are starting to grow. And when their kids want something sweet, they go out back and get honey from a beehive.

**Kristin Brennan:** There was this one hive, and they produced eighty pounds of honey this year, that we actually harvested. And then . . .

**Karen Brown:** Brennan and Staub are both thirty-one years old and college educated. Two years ago, they began a homesteading experiment. Now, they try to live a self-sufficient lifestyle. They produce almost all of their own food instead of shopping at the supermarket. They wear used clothes and shop at second-hand stores. They have no car, and instead bike, walk, or take the bus, whether they're going around town or visiting family in the next state. They don't use electricity in their house, either. They have candles for light and heat their home with wood.

**Daniel Staub:** We are attempting to live within a local economy. Locally-based economy is really about community for me, and it's about connection between people and each other, and the natural world around them.

**Karen Brown:** There is a long tradition of homesteading in the United States, but most homesteaders live in rural areas, on farms and in the countryside. What makes Brennan and Staub's lifestyle different is that they live in the middle of a poor, inner city neighborhood in Springfield, Massachusetts. They hope that other people will notice their simple lifestyle, and consider changing their own habits.

**Daniel Staub:** We could live this way anywhere. The question is, in what way will we be offering it most to people? A lot of people in a lot of different situations can benefit from changing their consumption habits . . .

**Karen Brown:** Since their move, they've worked hard to build relationships with neighbors. And they've gotten especially close to local children.

**Kristin Brennan:** Okay, so, you want to get as much of the root as you possibly can, so you're gonna kinda work around it, so let me show you, LJ.

**LJ:** Like this?

**Kristin Brennan:** No.

**Karen Brown:** Ten year old Lorenzo Nicholson is helping Brennan move plants from one part of the garden to another.

**Kristin Brennan:** . . . and you're gonna actually put your foot on top of the shovel.

**LJ:** I know.

**Kristin Brennan:** OK

**Karen Brown:** Lorenzo is one the young neighbors who enjoy spending most sunny afternoons in this backyard. However, the adults are harder to convince. Staub often tells family and friends that, even though it's more work, they enjoy their life this way. For instance, today they are sawing wood to burn in their wood stove.

**Daniel Staub:** If you see it as time that is taken away from, you know, something else that you really need to be doing, well, then it seems totally insane. But if you see it as something that is an activity worth doing in and of itself: you're getting exercise, you're spending time with family, you know, you're not using the fossil fuels that would be involved with using a chainsaw.

**Karen Brown:** While Brennan and Staub both believe in what they're doing, they still talk about how far to go. Brennan is usually more willing than her husband to put more wood on the fire when the house gets cold. And with two small children, she admits that she sometimes wants to use the clothes dryer that came with the house.

**Kristin Brennan:** And we've been tempted to throw diapers and covers into the dryer.

**Karen Brown:** And what stops you just before you do that?

**Kristin Brennan:** Well, I guess it's a slippery slope. We use the dryer once, maybe we'd be lured by the dryer again, and so, we decided not to do it.

**Karen Brown:** However, neither Brennan nor Staub wants to end their homesteading lifestyle. In fact, they hope to do more. Next year, they plan to buy a goat so they can have fresh milk. I'm Karen Brown.

## UNIT 8

### 1.1

**Woman's voice:** Good morning. This is Sarah and Mark on KWTP. This morning we need your opinion about marriage. But we're not just interested in what happens after you tie the knot. We want to know how you feel about what happens before the wedding.

### 1.2

**Woman's voice:** Good morning. This is Sarah and Mark on KWTP. This morning we need your opinion about marriage. But we're not just interested in what happens after you tie the knot. We want to know how you feel about what happens before the wedding.

**Mark:** That's right. You've all heard of prenuptial agreements. Well, call in and give us your opinion. Let the listeners know what you think of signing a prenuptial agreement before saying "I do."

Here's our first caller, Suzanne, from New York City. Hi, Suzanne. One question. Are you married?

**Suzanne:** I've been happily married now for ten years. But I have to admit there are times when I wish that my husband and I had signed some sort of contract before we got married. At the time, it didn't occur to me. You see, for the first two years we were married, John was the breadwinner, so it made sense that I would stay home and take care of the house. But now I'm a nurse and I work a 40-hour week too. Even so, John still expects me to cook all the meals. I do all the housework, too, and when I complain about it, he says, "I never told you to clean the house. It doesn't bother me if there's a little dust on the furniture." If I were going to do it all over, I'd make sure that we had an agreement to be equal partners in our marriage.

**Sarah:** OK, now let's hear from Amani, calling in from San Francisco.

**Amani:** I really don't think such an agreement would be possible in India, where I come from. One reason is that today many marriages are arranged by the couples' parents. The girl's parents try to find a husband who has a very good job. It is simply expected that the wife will stay home and take care of the house, while the husband earns the money. Actually, my husband and I didn't know each other until our parents' decided that we would be a good match. We have a very good life together. When we have a problem, we discuss it and work it out together.

**Mark:** That's wonderful! We have time for one more caller.

**Toshiyuko:** This is Toshiyuko and I'm calling in from Minneapolis. I agree with the caller from India. One reason my marriage works is that my wife and I keep many of the traditional Japanese roles. For example, my wife controls the family budget. Another reason is that we share many of the same interests. So we get along very well without any kind of written agreement.

**Mark:** That's all we have time for today. Thanks to everyone who called in. Have a great day!

## 1.3

**Speaker 1:** I'm glad you guys are happy, but I'd never sign a prenuptial agreement like this. No way. I don't care what you say; it's just not very romantic. I mean if you really love someone, you don't need to write all these things down. You just need to learn how to make your spouse happy and you've got to work out your problems right when they come up.

**Speaker 2:** I don't know about all this. . . . It might be a good idea, but the main problem is this contract has WAY too many details. Like the rule about going to sleep at 11:00 P.M. What if one person wasn't sleepy or wanted to watch the news or something? That would be breaking a rule, right? It's crazy. You can't plan every detail in your life. That's ridiculous!

## 3.2

Matt's wife will cook, and he will wash the dishes.
1. When Diana goes shopping for clothes, she always spends more money than planned.
2. Tim will vacuum the living room, if his mom asks him.
3. I wish my wife would sometimes prepare dinner for me.

## UNIT 9

### 1.1

**Speaker:** We're all here today for the same reason: we care about the environment. We care enough that we asked our elected officials to pass a law to preserve our atmosphere. This law would require businesses to reduce the amount of greenhouse gases they emit by a significant amount over the next ten years. However, it's not just big businesses that are responsible for the emissions of gases that contribute to global warming. We are all guilty of this crime against the environment. Therefore, it is up to each individual to contribute to a cleaner and healthier environment.

### 1.2

**Speaker:** We're all here today for the same reason: we care about the environment. We care enough that we asked our

elected officials to pass a law to preserve our atmosphere. This law would require businesses to reduce the amount of greenhouse gases they emit by a significant amount over the next ten years.

However, it's not just big businesses that are responsible for the emissions of gases that contribute to global warming. We are all guilty of this crime against the environment. Therefore, it is up to each individual to contribute to a cleaner and healthier environment. But you might wonder, "how can I have an impact?" "What can I do to offset the dangers that these invisible gases cause?

The answer is simple. You have to think about your own carbon footprint.

First, you must significantly decrease the amount of electricity you use. Do you really have to drive to the store when there's a bus that can take you? You don't really have to have the air conditioner running all summer, do you?

There are dozens of other ways to become more energy efficient:

For example, you must recycle all paper, plastic, and metal objects. If your community doesn't have a recycling plan, you will have to speak to your neighbors to put one in place.

If you have to drive to work, join a carpool.

If you don't have to drive to work, there are other simple alternatives. Try riding your bike or walking to work.

These are just a few things that you can do to reduce your carbon footprint.

And one more thing. Make sure your elected officials know that preserving the environment is important to you, and if they are smart, it will be important to them, too.

### 1.3

**Speaker:** We are here today because we want stop global warming. Like me, you're trying hard to reduce your own personal carbon footprint. And these small, individual changes do have an impact, do help lower our carbon emissions.

But it's not enough. It's not enough for individuals to change. We need governments to change. We need industry to change. We need big changes if we want to stop global warming from destroying our planet.

One third . . . one third of our global carbon emissions—35 percent—comes from producing electricity. We need government and industry to work together to lower these emissions. To develop new, cleaner technology to heat our homes, power our factories, and to keep the lights on.

Another twenty percent of our emissions comes from transportation. We need government and industry to work together to build more energy efficient cars and trucks. To build more public transportation. Good quality public transportation that will let us get rid of our cars and the pollution they produce forever!

# UNIT 10

## 1.1

**Announcer:** Clearly, we all agree that stealing is a crime, but what if the thief turns out to be a twelve-year-old girl? And what if it isn't the first time this sixth grader has been arrested for the very same crime? People are beginning to wonder, "Who's really responsible, the twelve-year-old girl, or her parents, for failing to properly discipline their child? Jenna Richards is in Dayton, Ohio, the scene of the crime.

## 1.2

**Announcer:** Clearly, we all agree that stealing is a crime, but what if the thief turns out to be a twelve-year-old girl? And what if it isn't the first time this sixth grader has been arrested for the very same crime? People are beginning to wonder, "Who's really responsible, the twelve-year-old girl, or her parents, for failing to properly discipline their child? Jenna Richards is in Dayton, Ohio, the scene of the crime.

**Reporter:** In Dayton, Ohio, this issue is big news. The Court has already made its decision. The judge says the parents of 12-year-old Jessica should be punished for their daughter's crime. Let's see what the people have to say about this decision.

Excuse me, sir, have you heard about the Court's judgment?

**Elderly man:** Yes, and I think it's about time. There's no doubt that parents are too permissive these days. They need to set limits on their children's behavior. I mean, parents let their children make the rules. Don't they understand that their children's misbehavior can have serious consequences?

**Reporter:** Thank you, sir. Uh, hello. I see you two have just come out of the courthouse.

**Young woman and young man:** Yes/We . . .

**Young woman:** We were watching the case because we work at the Jones Center for Family Causes. Our center teaches parents how to use problem solving to deal with family issues.

**Reporter:** And after watching the case, what do you think of the Court's decision?

**Young man:** Well, in most cases I think it's not a good idea to blame either the parents or the child. Our center advocates that both parents and children have rights and responsibilities. It seems that in Jessica's home, the parents were trying to keep their daughter out of trouble, but, at some point, they didn't have enough control over her actions.

**Reporter:** So it looks like the people's decision is split in this case. The controversy over this issue—should parents be punished for their child's actions—continues.

## 1.3

**Reporter:** Instead of spanking, Dr. Lau advocates problem solving and consequences as better ways to teach children life lessons.

**Beverly Lau:** Children learn best by doing. The best way to teach them how to behave is to get them to say what they did wrong and to think of what they should have done instead. We call this active problem solving and we need to show our children how to do it. There still needs to be a consequence for the misbehavior. But it should be a consequence that makes sense. Like "you hit your friend so we need to leave the playground." Or "you didn't finish your homework so you can't watch TV."

## 3.2

Some believe corporal punishment of children can lead to abuse.    Abuse
1. This couple hopes the counselor can give them helpful advice on how to deal with their daughter.    Advice
2. Modern parents try to raise their kids without spanking.    Raise
3. Psychologists say parents should use nonviolent methods of discipline.    Use
4. Our neighbor's son can run loose when his mother is not around.    Loose

# Achievement Tests Answer Key

## UNIT 1

### 1.1
B

### 1.2
1. C    2. D    3. B    4. A    5. D    6. A

### 1.3
1. memory pill
2. humorous/positive
3. humorous/positive

### 2.1
1. get our attention    3. fear    5. slogan
2. emotional    4. promote

### 2.2
1. A    2. D    3. C    4. C    5. D

### 3.1
1. have    3. introduces / is introducing
2. shakes / is shaking    4. looks

### 3.2
1. Wednesday    2. anniversary    3. Really?

### 3.3
1. A    2. D    3. C

### 4.1
A

### 4.2
Answers will vary.

### 4.3
Answers will vary. See the scoring rubric on page T-66.

## UNIT 2

### 1.1
B

### 1.2
1. C    2. B    3. D    4. D    5. A    6. A

### 1.3
1. E    2. F    3. B

### 2.1
1. Neither    3. Neither    5. Neither
2. Positive    4. Negative    6. Negative

### 2.2
1. products    3. criminal    5. avoid
2. accept    4. protected

### 3.1
1. B    2. C    3. C

### 3.2
1. credit    2. identity    3. check

### 3.3
1. And?
2. So, what happened next?
3. Wow!

### 4.1
A

### 4.2
Answers will vary. Suggested answers:

She should learn how to protect herself from identity theft.

She shouldn't leave her purse in the car again.

### 4.3
Answers will vary. See the scoring rubric on page T-66.

## UNIT 3

### 1.1
D

### 1.2
1. B    2. A    3. D    4. C    5. B    6. A

### 1.3
1. D    2. C    3. F

### 2.1
1. course    4. achieve
2. challenge    5. terrain
3. endurance

### 2.2
1. A    2. C    3. A    4. B    5. A

### 3.1
1. herself    3. myself
2. yourself    4. ourselves

### 3.2
1. the other night
2. each other
3. another

**3.3**

   **1.** S      **2.** W      **3.** S

**4.1**

Answers will vary. Suggested answers:

Be happy. It is a way of being wise.

Don't do whatever you like. Like whatever you do.

**4.2**

Answers will vary.

**4.3**

Answers will vary. See the scoring rubric on page T-66.

## UNIT 4

**1.1**

   D

**1.2**

   **1.** B      **2.** C      **3.** D      **4.** B      **5.** C      **6.** B

**1.3**

   **1.** Dialect      **2.** Dialect      **3.** Accent

**2.1**

   **1.** self-conscious
   **2.** make a big deal about
   **3.** fit in
   **4.** identity
   **5.** intentionally

**2.2**

   **1.** A      **2.** B      **3.** C      **4.** A      **5.** B

**3.1**

   **1.** couldn't      **2.** could      **3.** can      **4.** can't

**3.2**

   **1.** can      **2.** can't      **3.** can't

**3.3**

   **1.** Today I'd like to discuss what we mean by "accent" in speech.
   **2.** but let's get back to our discussion about accents.
   **3.** but I'm afraid that's all we have time for today.

**4.1**

Answers will vary. Suggested answer:

I would ask a question.

**4.2**

Answers will vary. Suggested answer:

I would not change topics too quickly.

**4.3**

Answers will vary. See the scoring rubric on page T-66.

## UNIT 5

**1.1**

   B

**1.2**

   **1.** A      **2.** C      **3.** C      **4.** B      **5.** D      **6.** A

**1.3**

   **1.** C      **2.** D      **3.** F

**2.1**

   **1.** E      **2.** C      **3.** A      **4.** B      **5.** D

**2.2**

   **1.** C      **2.** A      **3.** A      **4.** B      **5.** D

**3.1**

   **1.** wrap
   **2.** will not be able to/won't be able to
   **3.** will continue

**3.2**

   **1.** C      **2.** B      **3.** B      **4.** A

**3.3**

   **1.** definitely should not
   **2.** Let's
   **3.** We should

**4.1**

Answers will vary. Suggested answer:

We should tell people about the elephant controversy.

**4.2**

Answers will vary. Suggested answer:

We could make a contribution to Dumbo Express.

**4.3**

Answers will vary. See the scoring rubric on page T-66.

## UNIT 6

**1.1**

   D

**1.2**

   **1.** A      **2.** B      **3.** B

**1.3**

   **A.** 2      **C.** 4      **D.** 3

## 1.4

1. Go Back
2. Both
3. Lavender

## 2.1

1. approaching
2. whispered
3. driveway
4. repeated
5. scary

## 2.2

1. frightening
2. unattractive plants
3. friendly event
4. people at an event
5. expecting others to obey rules

## 3.1

1. to tell
2. try
3. to scare
4. to make

## 3.2

1. about
2. along
3. from

## 3.3

1. B
2. E
3. M

## 4.1

Answers will vary. Suggested answer: lonely

## 4.2

Answers will vary.

## 4.3

Answers will vary. See the scoring rubric on page T-66.

# UNIT 7

## 1.1

A

## 1.2

1. B
2. C
3. C
4. D
5. B
6. B

## 1.3

1. C
2. E
3. F

## 2.1

1. ashamed
2. take it easy
3. simple
4. gained
5. convinced

## 2.2

1. D
2. O
3. O
4. A/O
5. P/W

## 3.1

1. many
2. a few
3. a little more
4. a lot of

## 3.2

1. Did you get a lot of sleep last night?
2. He's under a lot of stress.
3. You need a day off.

## 3.3

1. quick
2. hot
3. brief

## 4.1

making coffee / taking it easy

## 4.2

This routine makes her feel happy or relaxed.

## 4.3

Answers will vary. See the scoring rubric on page T-66.

# UNIT 8

## 1.1

C

## 1.2

1. B
2. D
3. A
4. B
5. C

## 1.3

1. Not mentioned
2. Against
3. For
4. Against

## 2.1

1. G
2. C
3. I
4. F
5. D
6. H

## 2.2

1. before wedding day: propose
2. wedding day: tie the knot, become a spouse
3. marriage: be the breadwinner

## 3.1

1. happier than
2. not as windy as, less windy than
3. less crowded than, not as crowded as
4. more adventurous than

## 3.2

1. B
2. C
3. B

## 3.3

1. C or F
2. D
3. A

## 4.1

Answers will vary. Possible answer:

Married couples will fight less if they have a written agreement.

## 4.2

Answers will vary. Possible answer:

Married couples should be able to talk about their problems and find solutions.

## 4.3

Answers will vary. See the scoring rubric on page T-66.

# UNIT 9

## 1.1

   C

## 1.2

**1.** F   **2.** F   **3.** F   **4.** T   **5.** Not mentioned

## 1.3

People should use public transportation more.

## 2.1

1. emissions
2. significant
3. invisible
4. guilty
5. greenhouse gases

## 2.2

**1.** C   **2.** A   **3.** A   **4.** B   **5.** D

## 3.1

1. must not
2. can't
3. will have to
4. doesn't have to
5. don't have to

## 3.2

1. finished
2. finished
3. not finished
4. not finished
5. finished

## 4.1

A person's carbon footprint is his/her impact on global warming.

## 4.2

Answers will vary. Possible answer:

People must not keep appliances plugged in when not in use.

## 4.3

Answers will vary. See the scoring rubric on page T-66.

# UNIT 10

## 1.1

   B

## 1.2

**1.** C   **2.** C   **3.** B   **4.** C   **5.** B   **6.** A

## 1.3

**1.** Neither   **2.** Report about Jessica   **3.** Both

## 2.1

**1.** C   **3.** J   **5.** H   **7.** B
**2.** E   **4.** A   **6.** G

## 2.2

**1.** C   **2.** A   **3.** D

## 3.1

1. have . . . returned (alternative correct answer 've returned)
2. have . . . seen
3. Have . . . read
4. have spanked (alternative correct answer 've spanked)

## 3.2

1. /s/
2. /z/
3. /z/
4. /s/

## 3.3

**1.** C   **2.** B

## 4.1

Answers will vary.

## 4.2

Answers will vary.

## 4.3

Answers will vary. See the scoring rubric on page T-66.

# NorthStar 3 Achievement Test Scoring Rubric: Speaking

| Score | Description |
|-------|-------------|
| 4 | A response at this level demonstrates generally clear and automatic speech, with one or two short pauses and hesitations, and typically correct pronunciation of words; a response at this level is also marked by:<br>• mostly accurate information with logical connections to listening<br>• consistent use of complex grammatical features such as relative clauses, adverb phrases, and longer formulaic expressions<br>• use of multiple vocabulary words from and relevant to unit<br>• mostly accurate grammar and vocabulary use |
| 3 | A response at this level demonstrates generally clear and automatic speech, with one or two short pauses and hesitations, and generally correct pronunciation of words; a response at this level is also marked by:<br>• mostly accurate information with logical connections to listening<br>• somewhat consistent use of complex grammatical features such as relative clauses, adverb phrases, and longer formulaic expressions<br>• use of multiple vocabulary words from unit<br>• generally accurate grammar and vocabulary use |
| 2 | A response at this level demonstrates somewhat clear and automatic speech, with some short pauses and hesitations, and generally correct pronunciation of words; a response at this level is also marked by:<br>• generally accurate information with somewhat logical connection to listening<br>• consistent use of grammatical features such as prepositional phrases, modals, simple verb tenses, and direct objects; little or no attempt to use complex grammatical structures is made<br>• use of multiple vocabulary words from prompt<br>• generally accurate grammar and vocabulary use |
| 1 | A response at this level demonstrates somewhat clear and automatic speech, with multiple short pauses and hesitations, and some correct pronunciation of words; a response at this level is also marked by:<br>• generally accurate information with some connection to listening<br>• inconsistent use of grammatical features such as prepositional phrases, modals, simple verb tenses, and direct objects<br>• use of multiple vocabulary words from prompt<br>• somewhat noticeable errors in grammar and vocabulary use |
| 0 | A response at this level attempts to address the prompt in English, and is marked by long periods of silence or unintelligible speech; a response at this level is also marked by:<br>• information that is not connected to listening or lacks accuracy<br>• use of isolated words or short utterances<br>• very limited range of vocabulary; recycled prompt language<br>• frequent errors in grammar and vocabulary use<br>A response at this level could also include no attempt to respond. |

# Notes

# Notes

# Notes

# Notes

# Notes

# CD Tracking Guide
# Achievement Tests